English
Teaching as
Christian Mission

English Teaching as Christian Mission

An Applied Theology

Donald B. Snow

Herald Press

Scottdale, Pennsylvania
Waterloo, Ontario

Library of Congress Cataloging-in-Publication Data
Snow Donald B., 1954-
    English teaching as Christian mission : an applied theology / Don Snow.
        p. cm.
    Includes bibliographical references.
    ISBN 0-8361-9158-7 (alk. paper)
        1. Missions—Educational work. 2. English language–Study and teaching
    —Foreign speakers. I. Title

    BV2630 .S56 2001
    266'.02373—dc21   00-143893

ENGLISH TEACHING AS CHRISTIAN MISSION
Copyright © 2001 by Herald Press, Scottdale, Pa. 15683
        Published simultaneously in Canada by Herald Press,
        Waterloo, Ont. N2L 6H7. All rights reserved
Library of Congress Catalog Card Number: 00-143893
International Standard Book Number: 0-8361-9158-7
Printed in the United States of America
Cover design by Merrill Miller
Book design by Sandra Johnson

15 14 13 12 11   10 9 8 7 6 5 4

To order or request information, please call 1-800-245-7894, or visit
www.heraldpress.com.

To my parents,
for their understanding and support over many years

"And whatever you do, in word or deed,
do everything in the name of the Lord Jesus. . . ."
(Col. 3:17)

Contents

Foreword

I read many books every year, and the ones I usually enjoy the most are those on topics I myself have contemplated writing about, but which—once I finish reading them—leave me delighted that the author has succeeded in coming up with a much more thorough and finer piece of writing than I could have ever mustered. Such is the case with Don Snow's *English Teaching as Christian Mission: An Applied Theology*. In this work, he has managed to write thoughtfully, provocatively, and insightfully about the relationship between Christian faith and Christian praxis—specifically the practice of teaching English to nonnative speakers.

Some readers may have limited knowledge about teaching English to speakers of other languages (TESOL—the common acronym for this profession and itself the name of the world's largest language teachers organization), and they might wonder why someone would write a book about TESOL as a mission profession. After all, don't most missionaries serve as pastors, evangelists, or medical practitioners (as my own parents did first in China and then later in India)? Actually not. Among the many and enormous changes the world has witnessed over the last fifty years is the rise of English as the global language for nearly every facet of international communication (a point underscored in this book), and this linguistic transformation has had a significant impact on Christian mission. If we count all the short and long-term missionaries sent from the United States (a nation which some linguists call an "inner circle country," referring to the fact that English has served as both the dominant and the national language of that nation), it might be surprising to learn that the overt and official profession for the substantial majority of all these mission workers is teaching English. Indeed, there are several large interdenominational mission agencies in America whose sole (soul?) function is to recruit, train, send, and support thousands of teachers of TESOL as missionaries to other countries each year. On this basis alone, Don Snow's book is timely, for it justifies why it is just as important to have a missiological rationale for TESOL as it is for "traditional" missionary occupations such as evangelism or medical work.

But this book does not focus solely on missiology nor is it written exclusively for Christians, for Snow does a superb job of detailing how important it is for any TESOL professional to be sensitive, empathetic, and compassionate toward the non-native classroom learner. As implied by the sequencing of these terms, these special qualities of an ideal TESOL teacher ultimately lead to the Christian concept of reconciliation, and again the author argues persuasively for the potentiality for English teachers to become instruments of God's peace when they teach in a mission setting. But in addition to this Christian interpretation of TESOL, Snow provides many illustrations and arguments for how any English teacher can be more effective in a cross-cultural setting.

In my long career of training teachers in TESOL programs, my students have often been slow to appreciate the relevance of courses like second language acquisition or pedagogical grammar to their future careers, but I have persistently tried to emphasize that the main goal of these courses is to nourish within these student teachers empathy for the nonnative speakers they will be teaching. Ten years later, I could really care less whether any of my former students can define the recency effect, or can give me an example of an adjective which is always attributive and never predicative. Rather, the chief thing that I want them to come away with is a sense of awe about how anyone can ever learn any second language, or how miraculous it is that hundreds of millions of people all over the world have learned to converse so readily in English—a language whose grammar is so obtuse that even the brightest linguists still argue about its details. Sadly, native speakers of English who plunge into TESOL without any training or reflection often end up wondering why their students are so slow. And sadder still, many of these naïve English instructors teach in mission settings, supposedly as Christ's emissaries. A major contribution of this book then is to redefine the importance of compassion and reconciliation in the business of teaching English as Christian mission.

Years ago, after a flight to Toronto from the United States, I was questioned by an official at the Canadian immigration checkpoint. After the perfunctory question about my destination and the purpose of my visit, he asked me what I did, and without even thinking I casually replied that I was a professor. "Really?" he quickly responded, "and what do you profess?" The abrupt uniqueness of this query so startled me that I almost reacted as if I were in a catechism class and blurted out, "I profess Christ as my Lord and Savior!" But context and propriety overcame this fleeting instinct, and I came out with a sentence I had never said before. "I profess linguistics." It turned out he himself had had a few linguistics courses years before at university, so we enjoyed a few moments chatting about this arcane field before he finally waved me through. However, as I made my way into the airport, I couldn't help thinking about the remarkable way in which his unusual question provoked me to reflect on the relationship between my lifelong *profession* as a linguist and English language teacher and my lifetime commitment to Christ.

Up to that moment in my career, I had always associated the verb *professing* with my Christian faith but never with the noun and title *professor* which had defined my career and which describes my current job at a large and very secular urban university in California. There are other words which evoke this same conundrum. We talk of *calling on* students in class, but don't connect this to the idea of a *calling*. We talk about our *vocation*, but forget that this word is traditionally much more descriptive of theological issues than it is of teaching, or any other career choice for that matter. Historically and etymologically, *vocations* were a divine call to a career of ministry, like the call to the young Samuel, and related words also reveal its theological connotations (worship services begin with *invocations*; clergy meet at *convocations*, etc.). Nevertheless, when we use the word today, especially when asked what our *vocation* is, we rarely stop and reflect on the original and deeper meaning of this term.

Like the question posed by the Canadian immigration official, this book makes us stop and think reflectively and perhaps even prayerfully about how our jobs and careers as teachers of English as a foreign language are actually professions and vocations of our Christian beliefs. We know what our calling is, and as Christians, we know who is calling us, but *English Teaching as Christian Mission* tries to bridge the two by writing about how our calling can be a witness to who has called us. Teaching English is vital contribution to our students and is a substantive mission wherever we may be, but as Christian English teachers, hopefully we teach more than the language, and in doing that we have the opportunity to profess our faith.

—*Tom Scovel*
Walnut Creek, California   *June 10, 2000*

Preface

The questions addressed in this book have occupied me since 1983, when I first went abroad as an English teacher under the auspices of a Christian organization. However, the origins of this manuscript are more recent, lying in a short orientation program I conducted in the summer of 1995 for English teachers who were about to be sent abroad by the Presbyterian Church USA. All of these teachers had been through a general missionary orientation program, and I now had two days to better prepare them for the task of teaching English in foreign countries. As we discussed course planning, materials, methodology, classroom management, and so forth, I had a growing sense that something was missing, that we hadn't devoted enough attention to the link between English teaching and the call of Christian mission. When I raised my concern with the group toward the end of the second morning, they all quickly agreed that it was probably more important to spend our last afternoon together considering how English teaching relates to Christian mission than it was to go deeper into the nuts and bolts of teaching. The notes that I hastily scribbled down for that afternoon program became the first—albeit terribly rough—draft of this manuscript.

As I have attempted to carry this project forward from its humble beginnings, I have been blessed with invaluable assistance from many friends. A number of people have read the manuscript at various stages of its development, and their comments have resulted in many changes and improvements in this manuscript. I would like to express my gratitude to Dennette Alwine, Bud Carroll, Ian Groves, Sue Ellen Hall, Steve Henderson, John LeMond, Marian McClure, Michael Parker, Joseph Poulshock, Stephen Ting, Philip Wickeri, and Mary Shepard Wong. Special thanks to Kitty Purgason and Alan Seaman for both commenting on the manuscript and supplying me with valuable materials of which I would not otherwise have been aware. I also wish to thank Tom Scovel for not only commenting on the manuscript and writing a foreword, but also providing encouragement and sage advice through the course of this project. Naturally with such a diverse group of advisers, there are points on which we are not in full agreement, and final responsibility for what is written here is mine.

I would also like to thank Myrrl Byler, Todd Friesen, and other staff of China Educational Exchange for inviting me to air the ideas in this manuscript at their winter conference over the last several years, and to Scott Harris of the Maryknoll Fathers and Brothers for allowing me a similar opportunity at a conference of Maryknoll English teachers. The ensuing discussions were invaluable not only in helping me sort out my own thoughts but also in exposing me to a trove of new ideas from which I have borrowed shamelessly. Finally, I owe a debt of gratitude to the staff of the Amity Foundation, especially the Education Division, and the teachers who serve in China through Amity's Teacher Project. Unlike most organizations through which Christian English teachers go from Western countries to teach abroad, Amity is not a Western organization; instead, it is a Chinese nongovernment development organization established by Chinese Christians. Working with this organization over the past several years has helped me gain a better understanding of how the role and work of Christian English teachers looks from a non-Western perspective.

—*Don Snow*

1

A Christian Vocation
in Its Own Right

When we think about mission work, Western Christians are far more likely to think of pastors, evangelists, medical personnel, or even social service workers than we are of English teachers. However, English teachers have long played a significant role in the mission work of Western churches. Even in the early part of this century a survey conducted in preparation for the 1910 World Missionary Conference in Edinburgh found that "English language instruction was widespread in mission-sponsored educational institutions across the Far East, the Indian subcontinent, sub-Saharan Africa, and the Middle East."[1] Since that time, especially during the last several decades, a large and growing number of the personnel sent abroad by Western churches have been English teachers, and there are no signs of this trend abating. One recent book, *Handbook for Christian EFL Teachers,* lists more than sixty church or parachurch Christian organizations which regularly send English teachers abroad, not to mention more than twenty undergraduate and graduate programs in English teaching offered at Christian colleges and universities in the West.[2] I myself was first struck by the broader nature of this trend at a 1994 ceremony for new mission personnel being commissioned by the Presbyterian Church USA. As I counted my way through the placements and job descriptions of the people being sent, I discovered that over one fifth of these new mission workers were teachers of English, in this particular year being sent to places as diverse as China, Egypt, Ethiopia, Japan, Korea, Slovakia, and Thailand.

Given the number of Christians who work in mission as English teachers, it is surprising that there has not been more discussion within the church of this particular form of mission effort. After all, the role of English-teacher-as-missionary raises quite a few questions. One, for example, is the issue of how missionaries who work as English teachers balance dual roles as representatives of both Christianity and a Western language and culture. In the postcolonial era, this is an issue worthy of serious consideration.[3] Another issue is raised by the fact that in many countries it is the wealthy elite who are most likely to learn English. In such a situation, how do Christians respond to the Christian call to help the poor and oppressed—and to the possibility that their efforts may reinforce the power of the privileged members of society?

However, perhaps the most fundamental issue is that of how English teaching relates to Christian service and mission. In what way does English teaching become Christian vocation, as opposed to a useful but ultimately secular service? For different people this issue may take a variety of forms, but the two examples below are both illustrative and typical of the difficulties Christians may encounter in attempting to integrate English teaching and mission.

1. The mission tradition of Christians from conservative or evangelical backgrounds tends to emphasize evangelistic outreach, and Christian English teachers from this background often assess the value of their mission work at least partly on the basis of whether or not any of their students become Christians. Within this tradition, English teaching is seen as a useful mission vehicle in part because Christian English teachers have the opportunity to live and work in countries which for religious, political, or cultural reasons do not accept missionaries who openly work as evangelists, pastors, or in other church-related capacities. English teaching is also a useful approach to mission because English is a

valuable commodity which attracts an audience. In many countries, people who would never go to an evangelistic meeting conducted in their own language will tolerate the gospel when presented in English simply because it gives them a chance to practice their English skills. Within this mission tradition, English teaching often starts out as a means to an end rather than an end in itself, and while this does not necessarily mean that Christian teachers are not serious about their teaching work, there is a potential gap between the English teacher and missionary aspects of the role.

One problem sometimes created by this gap is doubt as to the ultimate value of the many hours put into classroom teaching, lesson planning, and grading of homework assignments. For missionaries working as English teachers, the duties involved in language teaching consume a great deal of time, and if teachers do not see all those hours invested in teaching as hours spent in God's service it is easy for them to become discouraged and to feel that they are not really following God's call. This is especially true if the investment doesn't generate many opportunities for them to explicitly share their faith with students.

Another problem created by a gap between the teacher and missionary roles is difficulty in articulating one's mission to supporting churches and Christians in the home country. When the sending community judges the value of a missionary's work largely in terms of how many churches are planted or how many people become Christians, it can be difficult for a Christian English teacher to explain the value of his or her work. In a worst case scenario, this may result in pressure on Christian English teachers to exaggerate the amount of interest in Christianity their work generates, or to produce a certain number of conversions to satisfy the sending church. It might even result in a home church community or sending agency being unwilling to support the work of a Christian English teacher unless there is evidence that it produces conversions. More often, the problem is a nagging sense in either the missionary or the support community that work as a

Christian English teacher is not quite "real" missionary work, and that the value of work done by Christian English teachers is somehow a discounted form of mission. In short, the gap between language teaching and Christian mission may result in both the teacher and the supporting community failing to experience the fullness of God's call for work as a Christian English teacher.

2. In mainline or liberal Christian traditions, problems with the idea of English teaching as Christian mission are rather different. In their thinking about mission, Christians in mainline churches tend to emphasize Christian service, especially to the poor and oppressed, more than evangelism. The problem with English teaching is that it doesn't seem to be a mission of compassion in the way that disaster relief or poverty alleviation are, especially if students are middle or even upper class. As a result, English teachers may be viewed as a lesser form of mission. The problem is exacerbated by difficulty in defining what is distinctively Christian about the work of Christian English teachers. For example, one typical setting for Christian English teachers from mainline churches would be a school overseas that was originally started by that church and with which the church still maintains close ties. The Christian origins of such schools are often still apparent in one way or another, but the staff and students may not be predominantly Christian, and often the general ethos does not differ dramatically from local government-run schools. Another typical setting might be in a church-run community center in the United States which provides language classes for new immigrants or refugees. Again, while such centers provide much-needed services in an atmosphere of Christian compassion, the English classes may be quite similar to those offered by community centers sponsored by nonchurch groups.

In settings such as those above, the value of English teaching is generally not in question, but it can be hard to see what if anything distinguishes a teacher in such an environment from a Peace Corps worker or a non-Christian community volunteer. Thus, while in mainline churches there is generally a sense that English teaching is a nice thing to do, questions may be raised as to how high a priority churches should give to it, especially when increasing financial diffi-culties are forcing churches to critically examine their prior-ities and articulate more clearly their rationales for the kinds of mission which they support.

This book explores the relationship of Christian mission to English teaching, arguing that English teaching can and should be Christian vocation in its own right, not simply a means to other ends or a secular task only incidentally engaged in by Christians. The main focus of this book is not on how English teaching can serve as a vehicle for evange-lism, although I believe that much of what I say will help Christian English teachers be more effective as witnesses to the Christian faith. Neither is my primary concern with English teaching in and of itself, although again I hope that what I say will help Christian English teachers be more effec-tive as language teaching professionals. My main concern is rather with the territory in between these two positions, with the variety of ways in which Christian English teachers can integrate the Christian and educational aspects of their work as a whole.

I do not assume that Christian English teachers must always seek full integration between their language teaching and Christian service. There are, for example, situations where missionaries teach English simply in order to have financial support for other kinds of mission work. However, I believe that being able to see one's teaching work as Christian service in its own right and being able to articulate that connection is beneficial to both the Christian teacher and the work. The issue of *how* to teach will enter the dis-cussion at various points, and I will argue in the following chapters that some choices as to who, where, and how to teach are easier to reconcile with Christian mission than oth-ers. However, we will more often be exploring possible answers to the question *why* Christians should be engaged in English teaching. My hope is that this book will help Christian English teachers, church administrators, and lay people concerned with mission more effectively articulate to themselves and others the ways in which English teaching can be Christian service and mission.

My focus in this book will be almost exclusively on Western Christian English teachers who work overseas, a group which I will refer to as "Christian English Teachers" or, for the sake of convenience, "CETs." In order to have a comprehensive picture of the role of English teaching in Christian mission, it would also be necessary to consider the countless professional and volunteer Christian English teachers who teach refugees, immigrants, and international students and their spouses in churches, schools, and community centers in English-speaking countries. However, due to the limitations of my own experience I have chosen to focus on the overseas experience. (To Christian English teachers in other settings I offer my apologies, and my hope that much of what is said here will still be relevant to their work.) I should also note that the audience I have most often in mind is those CETs who are either preparing for or engaged in short-to-medium length terms of service abroad (periods ranging from one to five years), or who are in the early stages of a longer term. Readers will also no doubt notice I tend to refer disproportionately to China, and to settings where teachers work with adult students in college-level settings. This reflects the limits of my own experience, but the setting it reflects is also typical of those in which many CETs work.[4]

As should be clear by this point, I am attempting the ambitious and rather tricky task of addressing a very broad Christian audience, ranging in theological background from conservative-evangelical to mainline to liberal. Needless to say, within this range there are very different opinions as to what Christian mission should consist of, and my own assumptions cannot possibly always be identical to those of all readers. There is also a huge range of different contexts in which mission efforts take place, and no single discussion can be fully informed by all the different settings in which English teachers try to work out their Christian call. It may thus be of benefit to readers to have some idea of what experiences inform and shape my own views and approach.

My Christian background is something of a mixed bag; growing up in Presbyterian and Reformed churches, but also involved with Young Life, Inter-Varsity, a variety of campus fellowships, and independent community churches. My experience of volunteer and professional Christian service has been predominantly overseas as a language teacher in Taiwan, mainland China, and Hong Kong, working for a number of different Christian and church-related organizations including the YMCA, Educational Services Exchange with China (now Educational Services International), United Board for Higher Education in Asia, the Amity Foundation, and the Presbyterian Church (USA). This background helps account both for my focus on overseas work rather than Christian mission at home, and for my interest in trying to address a rather wide segment of the Christian mission community.

The fact that the bulk of my experience has been in China has no doubt significantly affected my view of how English teaching relates to Christian service. In China Christianity is often seen as a foreign religion and there is still resistance to Christianity because of its association with the West. The Chinese government does not permit traditional Western missionaries to work in the country, and by law foreigners are not allowed to carry out evangelistic activities. These realities have compelled me to spend much time considering the non-evangelistic aspects of English teaching as Christian service, perhaps more than would have been the case with someone whose experience was in countries without such prohibitions. My China experience has also made me especially sensitive to the ways in which the historic link between Christianity and the West affects mission efforts by Christians from Western nations.

The situation in China is undoubtedly different in many ways from that in other countries to which CETs may go, and there may be places in this book where my experience in China has led me to conclusions that would not apply so well in other countries. However, on the whole I suspect that the directions in which my China experience have pushed my thinking have been more helpful than not. In its experience of the West as colonial power and adversary, China is more typical of non-Western nations than exceptional, and the wariness of the Chinese government toward Western Christians is not unusual for governments in many countries, especially socialist or Islamic. In my discussions with CETs who work in other parts of the world, even places as distant from China as Africa and Latin America, my experience has been that there are often significant similarities in the kinds of issues CETs face.

One difficulty in discussing the work of CETs arises from the fact that the sending of English teachers is such a predominantly Western type of mission. When it comes to English teachers in mission, both the sending organizations and missionaries themselves are almost always Western, and churches in the host country too often play little part in the relationships through which Christian English teachers go abroad. The primary receiving organizations for Western CETs are often government or private schools that have no tie to the church. The result is that as we focus on this kind of mission, it is easy for our thinking to slip back toward older paradigms in which it was assumed that Western churches always played the sending role and the role of other nations was to be passive recipients. I hope the following chapters will make it clear that this is not a paradigm I wish to promote. Lest there be any misunderstanding, I wish to state clearly at the start that the type of mission under discussion in this book—the work of Christian English teachers—is not normative for Christian mission as a whole. Rather it is but one small and rather unique part of the work of the church. I will also argue that while the peculiarly Western nature of this type of mission is potentially a weakness, it is also in its intimate tie with the West that this particular form of mission may find its special role in the broader mission work of the church universal.

In conclusion, I should note a debt to recent books such

as Mark Noll's *The Scandal of the Evangelical Mind* and George Marsden's *The Outrageous Idea of Christian Scholarship*[5] which underscore the need for Christians to love God with their minds as well as their hearts. These books also suggest that this love needs to take the form of careful consideration, from a Christian perspective, of all aspects of life, not merely those which seem obviously religious or spiritual. If we are going to teach English—or do anything else—as service to God, it seems only right that we should give the matter deep and prayerful thought.

2

A Special Role for
Christian English Teachers?

The growth of English teaching in the mission work of Western churches has resulted in large part from the laws of supply and demand. On the supply side of the equation, in Western countries it is relatively easy to recruit people who are willing and able to serve as English teachers. Many English-speaking missionaries and lay tent-makers (in the spirit of the apostle Paul) are able to secure English teaching jobs solely on the basis of their native skills in English. This means that there are far more potential English teachers in Western churches than there are pastors, nurses, and other types of professionals who might be employed in mission work. Of course only a limited number of people are trained teachers of English as a foreign language, and there is considerable merit to the argument that Christian English teachers (CETs) should have professional training in language pedagogy. Such training is especially important if, as I believe is necessary, we view the quality of CETs' work as an important part of their witness. (See chapter 4 for further discussion.) On the other hand, however, it is true that a relatively short training course can generally enable a native speaker of English to perform credibly as a teacher of English conversation.

On the demand side of the equation, the dominant role played by English as the world's international language of business, diplomacy, and scholarship has generated a great need for English teachers worldwide. English is a required subject in the state school systems of many nations, thus providing employment for large numbers of Western English teachers. In many nations there are also numerous private schools catering to the needs of individuals who desire English skills for work, education, or social life. In both state and private schools, native speakers of English are highly valued not only for their language and culture background, but also because their presence makes English study seem much more real and exciting to students and does much to enhance students' levels of motivation and interest. For these reasons, it is possible for CETs to secure jobs almost anywhere in the world.

Much of the growth in recruitment of CETs by Western church and parachurch sending agencies is fueled by the fact that it is often possible for CETs to get jobs and work visas in countries where Western missionaries are generally not welcomed. This is especially true in Communist, recently ex-Communist, or Muslim nations.[1] The demand for English teachers is such that nations which would not normally allow the presence of Western missionaries will often employ English teachers from Christian church or parachurch agencies. It is often implied or made explicitly clear, however, that CETs are expected to function as secular workers rather than missionaries, and there are often restrictions on the kinds of religious activities CETs can engage in even outside the classroom. Nevertheless, whether their presence is welcomed or just tolerated, the fact is that CETs often have the opportunity to live and work in countries where there are few other Western Christians—or perhaps even few other Christians of any kind.

Supply and demand factors help explain the growth of English teaching as a kind of mission, but in and of themselves they don't constitute a missiology. If CETs and their sending church communities are to experience the full significance of their work, we should look beyond such factors and consider how the work of CETs from Western nations might fit into the broader mission work of the church universal. However, before addressing this question I should explicitly state several assumptions I make about the nature of Christian mission.

We should start with the idea that mission is not activity undertaken by individual Christians on their own initiative. Rather it is "missio Dei"—the mission of God. The word "mission" derives from a Latin word meaning "to send," and as Wilbert Shenk notes, mission involves "being sent with a commission to perform a certain task, acting in the name of a superior, carrying out an important mandate, serving as ambassador on behalf of one's leader."[2] The impetus for mission does not derive from individual Christians or Christian churches, but rather, is an activity initiated by God in which the church participates. As God the Father sent the Son to the world, and the Son sent the Spirit, so the Triune God sent the church into the world as an instrument for mission.[3] Such an understanding of mission is reflected in 1 Corinthians 3:6-9. Here Paul describes the founding of the church in Corinth as a process whereby he planted the seed and the evangelist Apollos watered it, but it was God who gave growth to the church. The work itself was of God, not of human hands, and Paul and Apollos were but God's workers.

A second thing that is clear from the Corinthians passage cited above is that Paul does not view his work as that of a single individual working directly under God's direction. Rather, he views his work in the broader context of the work of God's church, a work in which he played just one small part. The role of the church in mission is also seen in Acts 13:1-3 when Paul and Barnabas were called to a special work of God by the Holy Spirit. The call was heard through the church in Antioch, and it was the Antioch church which sent the pair off on their first mission. This pattern continues through Paul's career as he works in partnership with other Christian mission workers such as Silas, Apollos, and Timothy, with Christian churches in many cities, and with church leaders in Jerusalem.

One implication of both the "missio Dei" concept and Paul's example is that any discussion of mission needs to take place within the context of the church, and needs to be based on an understanding of its nature. In 1 Corinthians 12, Paul describes the church as a body of many different parts, each part having its own distinct role. As the body is composed of different parts—hands, feet, eyes—all having important but different roles in the functioning of the body as a whole, likewise within the church there are a variety of different roles, among which he mentions apostles, prophets, miracle workers, healers, helpers, administrators, and speakers of tongues. If we assume that God's mission is carried out by the church—the body of Christ on earth—and if each part of the body has its own unique function, it seems reasonable to ask whether or not English teachers might have a special role to play in the body of Christ and the mission of God. I will argue throughout this book that CETs do indeed have such a special role, but in order to understand this role we need first to look more closely at the unique nature of both CETs' work and the contexts within which they work.

Mission and English Teaching

According to the view of mission presented above, CETs are ambassadors of God and the church. However, it would be unrealistic not to recognize that the nature of their work also makes CETs ambassadors of the West to a degree which is arguably greater than is true of other kinds of Western mission personnel. As Paul Hiebert notes, people in other countries generally view Western missionaries primarily as representatives of their countries, and only secondarily as missionaries.[4] This is so in part because the great majority of CETs are necessarily Westerners from the United States, the United Kingdom, or other English-speaking Western nations. The identification of CETs with the West is also especially strong because, as English teachers, CETs are daily involved in the task of promoting the West's most widely used language and teaching the culture of its most powerful nations. This virtually ensures that no matter how CETs view themselves, in the host culture they will be seen as ambassadors of the West. CETs may have mixed feelings about this role. Some would embrace it willingly, while others might even resent it. However, it would be unrealistic for either CETs or their sending agencies not to accept the fact that this is an inherent part of CETs' work.

We also need to recognize that to the extent CETs are perceived in their host countries as ambassadors of the church, they are primarily seen as ambassadors of *Western* churches. In part, this is a legacy of history. People around the world are accustomed to an order of things in which Western churches send missionaries to receiving countries elsewhere, so it is simply assumed that CETs represent Western churches and Western churches only. However, this assumption is reinforced when, as is often the case, CETs have no institutional ties to local churches in the host country. As noted in chapter 1, English teaching is a form of mission engaged in mainly by Western churches. Even in countries where local Christian churches and groups exist they are often not much involved in the process by which CETs serve in their countries. This is not always true, and some CETs do serve abroad under joint arrangements between a sending agency in their home country and a church or Christian agency in their host country. Such arrangements are more common among denominational church mission programs which have close ties with sister churches in the host country. However, for many CETs, especially tent-makers or those sent by parachurch organizations, the only institutional tie in the host country is to a state or private (usually secular) school, so there is no visible link in the host country which would suggest that a CET in any way represents a local Christian body.

Sometimes this lack of ties with local Christian bodies results from necessity. CETs often serve in countries where local Christian groups would be unwilling or unable to engage in joint sponsorship of Western CETs, or where potential church partners simply do not exist. It also sometimes results from a lack of willingness on the part of Western sending agencies to work in partnership with local Christians, either because Western groups don't understand or trust local Christian groups, or because such partnership is generally more complicated and difficult than arrangements involving fewer parties, or because Western groups are reluctant to give up a portion of their decision-making authority. However, whatever the reason, this lack of institutional ties to churches in the host country tends to underscore the identification of most CETs with Western churches.

This uniquely strong identification of CETs with the West and Western Christianity is significant because the kinds of nations in which CETs are most likely to work, sometimes referred to in Western mission circles as "limited access countries," are generally nations that have very mixed feelings about both the West and Western Christianity. In fact, these countries offer only limited access to Westerners and Western Christians precisely because past relations with the West and its churches have often been difficult. In order to understand what special calling CETs might have in mission, next we need to consider the contexts in which they work and the legacies that they inherit.

The CET Mission Context
The legacy of the West

As representatives of Western nations and teachers of the most dominant Western language, the way CETs and their role are viewed by people in their host countries is inevitably affected by the past experiences of those people with the West and Westerners. While it is far beyond the scope of this book to recount in any detail the story of how the West—or Christendom, as it was once called—came to dominate the world stage, a brief summary is necessary.

It was not because of any inherent linguistic superiority that English achieved the role of the world's preeminent international language. Rather, the rise of English is due to the enormous political, military, economic, and cultural influence that English-speaking nations—first the United Kingdom and then the United States—have wielded throughout the world for the last two hundred years. Great Britain became the West's leading power in the early 1800s after the defeat of Napoleon's France, and by the end of the century it had a worldwide empire of colonies and spheres of economic and political influence that stretched all the way through Africa, the Middle East, South Asia, East Asia, and North and South America. With the decline of the British Empire in this century, particularly after the Second World War, the United States succeeded Britain as the West's leading power. During the era of the Cold War, the dominance of the West was challenged by the Soviet Union and its allies, but with the disintegration of the Soviet bloc and even the Soviet Union itself, the United States emerged as the world's pre-eminent military, economic, and cultural power.[5]

Over the last two centuries "Anglo-America," as one recent writer describes the paired English-speaking powers,[6] has been uniquely successful in projecting military, industrial, economic, political, and cultural influence throughout the world. Because of this, while the experiences nations around the world have had historically with Anglo-America vary considerably, there are two generalizations we can safely make. The first is that English-speaking diplomats, soldiers, traders, missionaries, and even tourists have visited virtually every corner of the globe, so any place where a CET might work almost certainly has a long legacy of contact with the West. The second is that during the last century virtually all countries in which CETs work have experienced some form of domination at the hands of Western nations—often either Britain or the United States.

Because these two English-speaking countries have generally dealt with other nations from a position of strength, they have been able to impose their will on other nations and peoples in a variety of ways. Some nations were conquered and colonized outright. As noted above, during much of the nineteenth and twentieth centuries Britain had an empire of colonies that literally circled the world.[7] While the United States was less active as a colonizer outside its own continental borders, it also set up colonial regimes in several countries (notably the Philippines) during the early twentieth century.

Many nations which were never actually colonized by either Britain or the United States were forced to offer trade concessions or accept a high degree of British or American economic and political influence. One of the best known examples of this is the Opium War, through which Britain forced China to accept British opium imports, open more ports to Western trade, and allow Westerners—including missionaries—rights of residence in China.[8] For the United States, examples of such policies would include a long series of military interventions in the politics and economics of Central and Latin America, as well as the sailing of the U.S. fleet into Japan's Edo Bay in 1853, a show of force which resulted in Japan's opening to trade with the West.

Other nations were defeated by Britain and the United States in political, military, or economic rivalry. While the example of this most relevant to CETs would be the recent collapse of the Soviet Union, this category also encompasses the experiences of Japan and Germany after World War II. Finally, many nations sense that their cultures are threatened by the world domination of Western culture, particularly the English-speaking American variety which is exported so successfully by Hollywood in the form of films and television programs. While this form of "domination" is not backed up by force the way other forms have been, the economic power of the United States makes its media culture difficult to compete with. This cultural influence is often viewed by other nations—even other Western nations—as a form of American cultural imperialism.

My point in this overview is not that the United States and Britain have been especially evil in their exercise of power. On the whole their use of power has probably been no more onerous than that of other nations which have had the opportunity to wield similar levels of power. Nor do I intend to imply that the English-speaking powers of the West are universally hated—the picture is more complex than that. The feelings of non-Western people toward Westerners vary considerably from one country to the next. In some countries there is unconcealed hostility toward the West, often with the United States playing the leading role as the "Great Satan," and grievances are nurtured in history books, the media, and public discourse. In other countries the wounds of history are healed to the extent that they are not evident unless irritated, and people have more positive attitudes toward the West, often being attracted to the West's material prosperity, popular culture, and individual freedoms.

My point is rather to emphasize that in virtually all of the countries where CETs are most likely to teach, there is a legacy of very mixed feelings toward the West, particularly now toward the United States. Respect and admiration for the achievements of the West are often mixed with envy of its success and resentment at its exercise of power. Even in countries where CETs encounter little overt anti-Western sentiment, there is often latent resentment toward Western power.

One issue worthy of special mention is the bitterness people in many countries feel toward the attitudes of superiority Westerners have often exhibited toward other cultures. As Paul Hiebert notes, during the period of Western colonial expansion: "Few Westerners took other cultures seriously or sought to understand them in their own terms. Many Westerners saw themselves as superior to the peoples they met."[9] Given the unprecedented achievements of the English-speaking West over the last two centuries, especially in areas such as technological and scientific progress, a Western sense of confidence and pride is understandable. However, the attitude with which Westerners have approached other cultures has often gone further than that, even extending to a belief that Western culture is synonymous with all that is modern and good, and that the cultures of other nations are inferior. This attitude is a source of resentment in countries the world over. No matter how poor or under-developed they may seem to be by Western standards, people virtually always take pride in their own cultures (although this is often mixed with a sense of inferiority or failure due to relative lack of development). Among many of the peoples and cultures of the world, resentment toward the attitudes of superiority is one of the most painful legacies of their experience with the English-speaking West.

A caveat: Even where hostility toward the West exists, it is not always something that CETs will encounter personally, and it most certainly does not necessarily translate into lack of enthusiasm for learning English. English has become an international language which is associated in the minds of many with modernity as much as with any particular nation or culture. As Alan Seaman points out, in today's world English is generally taught because people in the host nation demand it rather than because it is forced on them by a colonial government.[10] However, in parts of the world where people do have mixed or hostile feelings about the English-speaking powers, students may feel caught between the utilitarian benefits of learning English and a dislike for what it stands for. This is especially true in many Muslim areas of the Middle East, or in socialist (or ex-socialist) countries which have a history of adversary relations with the capitalist West. In other parts of the world, students may be more favorably inclined toward English and Western culture, but also sensitive to any suggestion that the West and its premier language are somehow inherently superior to their own language and culture. This would be the case in much of Asia and Eastern Europe, where English is generally studied enthusiastically but where there is also often a reservoir of wounded pride.

A final point that deserves mention here concerns the impact of Western power and dominance on other nations' sense of identity. One of the most potent factors in helping a group develop a strong sense of identity is struggle with a competitor, an "other" against which the group can define itself. In many nations colonized by the West, it was only during struggle against the colonial overlords that a modern sense of national identity developed, and the sense of identity created in such circumstances tended to emphasize differences between local culture and the culture of the Western colonial power. The result is that in many countries, even those which have actually borrowed many elements of modern Western culture, there is a strong sense of the West as "other," a sense that it is not possible to drink too deeply from the Western well without losing one's own heritage and identity. Even in nations which were never colonized by the West, the national sense of identity was forged in part by contrasting their culture with the culture of the West. A good example of this is Russia, which often highlights its Orthodox and Asian elements to contrast its culture with that of the West. This phenomenon is of relevance to CETs because, as we shall see below, it has had a significant impact on the attitude of many cultures toward the Christian faith.

Christianity and the West

A second aspect of the historical legacy CETs inherit concerns how people in host countries view Christianity. In many of the nations to which CETs go, Christianity is closely associated in the popular mind with the West. In fact, it is often assumed that all Westerners are by definition Christian. In the Muslim world of North Africa and the Middle East, this tendency to associate Christianity (at least its Western versions) with the West is ancient and deep. In fact, the two are often assumed to be one and the same.[11] In many parts of Africa and Asia the association is more recent but no less strong. The missionaries who introduced Christianity to these countries, or at least made it more widely known there, were Westerners. Furthermore, the appearance of these Western missionaries coincided with the appearance of Western soldiers and traders (generally calling themselves Christians), and the missionaries were often on close terms with these other Westerners. While some Western missionaries distinguished themselves from Western political or economic interests by championing the interests of local people—even when those interests conflicted with those of their home countries—other missionaries actively or passively collaborated with imperialist actions in the hope that Western domination of other nations would make it easier for missionaries to penetrate these nations to preach the gospel.[12]

We need to recognize much that was good in Western mission efforts over the last several centuries. Western missionaries made a significant contribution toward bettering life in many of the nations where they worked, and their lives often made a positive impact on those who came to know them. Furthermore, the efforts of Western missionaries resulted in the establishment and growth of Christian churches, many of which have long since become independent of their Western parent churches. In fact, one of the most amazing stories of the past few decades has been the way in which Christianity has spread in many parts of the non-Western world (at the same time it is declining in some of the former sending nations of the West).

However, we also need to recognize that in many nations the close tie between Christianity and the West resulted in negative feelings toward Christianity. For local people, awareness of God's love as lived out by Western missionaries is often overshadowed by awareness of the power of the nations from which the missionaries came, and sometimes even of the threat of force which enabled the Western missionaries to be there at all. As Ajith Fernando, Sri Lanka's director of Youth for Christ, writes: "Our concerted efforts to get people to separate Western political powers from the Christian enterprise do not have much success. The opponents of evangelism keep reminding us of this era when 'Christian' countries dominated us not for our benefit, but for their national interest."[13]

In nations which were invaded, colonized, or economically dominated by Western countries, the work of Western missionaries was sometimes seen as part of an assault on the local culture. The fact that some Western missionaries shared general Western attitudes toward the people and cultures in which they worked, viewing themselves as superior and looking down on the "poor heathen," further distanced Christianity from local people.[14] Even where relations between Western missionaries and local people were relatively good, the association of Christianity with the West meant that as nationalist, anticolonialist, and independence movements developed in nations dominated by Western powers, a local person who became Christian was often seen as abandoning his or her own culture and nation. This sense is perhaps summed up in a slogan of the anti-Christian movement among Chinese students and intellectuals in the 1920s—"One more Christian, one less Chinese." Conflict defined identities and hardened lines of division, creating a stronger sense of "us" and "them," and Christianity was defined as "theirs." (It is probably no accident that the Asian nation in which Protestant Christianity grew the most was Korea, which was colonized by Japan instead of by a Western nation.)

To keep things in perspective, I should again note that it may not always be immediately evident to CETs that this association of Christianity with the West has the potential to alienate non-Western people from it. In fact, CETs in some countries may discover that some people become interested in Christianity precisely because of its important role in Western culture. At the level of daily experience, therefore, CETs may not sense this perceived tie between Christianity and the West to be disadvantageous to either. This is especially true because CETs generally work with people who are inclined to be interested in the West. Also, CETs are often treated as guests, and people in many cultures feel an obligation to be polite and not share rude or hostile feelings they have about a CET's nation or culture. However, in many nations, even today this sense that Christianity is a foreign or Western religion is a burden for local churches and an obstacle to their growth.

Western Christians and other churches

I wish to briefly mention a third legacy which CETs will inherit in some countries, a history of strained or even hostile relations between local and Western Christians. In some countries the problem has been one of poor relations between Western missionaries and ancient non-Western

Christian churches (such as the traditional Orthodox churches of the Middle East). In many countries Western missionaries made little attempt to build relations with these older non-Western churches. As Norman Horner suggests, the non-Western churches tended to view Western missionaries as "sheep stealers" who built their churches by bringing in members mainly from the non-Western Christian population rather than from among the non-Christian population.[15] For Western missionaries working in traditionally Orthodox areas such as Russia and other parts of Eastern Europe, the potential today for similar problems is very real.

In other places the problem is one of damaged relations between Western churches and local churches that were originally founded by Western missionaries. After founding churches in other nations, Western missionaries were often slow to hand over control to local Christians. Leadership and decision-making authority sometimes remained in Western hands for decades after it should have been handed over. In many cases this continued Western control arose from a genuine sense that continued Western support and guidance were in the best interests of the daughter church, but often these good intentions were based on the unconscious or even explicit assumption that Western Christians were superior to their local brethren. In too many places an unintended consequence of this parental approach was that continued Western dominance came to be seen by local Christians as evidence that Western Christians didn't fully trust them or consider them equals.

Unfortunately attitudes of superiority on the part of Western Christians are not entirely a thing of the past. Among many Western Christians even today there is still a lingering (though often subconscious) assumption that despite its obvious problems Western Christianity is somehow truer than the Christianity practiced by non-Western people, and that indigenous Christians and their churches are less mature than—or even inferior to—their Western counterparts. Naturally this assumption is often resented by non-Western Christians, and provides a sore point in relations between churches of the West and churches elsewhere. In some countries, the issue is so sensitive that local Christians are forced to distance themselves from Western Christians in order to assert their independence and identity as mature churches.

A Special Role for CETs

Some CETs may question whether the legacy of the past discussed above has much relevance for CETs today; I experienced such questions from a number of Western participants at one recent conference for CETs. However, the participants of this particular conference included (somewhat atypically) several CETs who were Asian, and they were unanimously adamant that this history of Western domination was vitally important for Western CETs to both know about and be sensitive to. My own sense is that there is more danger of CETs paying too little attention to the past, and to their dual role as ambassadors of the church and of the West, than in paying it too much attention. CETs who are not sensitive to this legacy may inadvertently rub salt in wounds rather than helping heal them. This is particularly true for CETs who have little interest in the local culture and language, those who feel strongly that their own culture is superior to that of the host country, and those who tend not to distinguish between Christian faith and Western culture.

However, I also feel that it is in their unique association with Western culture and the Western church that CETs special calling in mission lies. There are certainly a variety of important ways in which CETs can serve the church, and in the following chapters we will consider a number of these: witness through life and work, ministry to the needs of students, service to the disadvantaged, promoting better intercultural understanding, and bridge-building between churches of different cultures. But, I would also argue that the special way in which CETs serve as ambassadors of both the church and the West gives them a special calling to a work of reconciliation.

Scripture consistently describes reconciliation as being at the very core of God's mission to humankind, carried out through the person of Jesus Christ. Scripture also clearly states that this mission of reconciliation has been passed on to the church. As Paul writes: "All this is from God, who reconciled us to himself through Christ, and has given us the ministry of reconciliation; that is, in Christ God was reconciling the world to himself, not counting their trespasses against them, and entrusting the message of reconciliation to us. So we are ambassadors for Christ, since God is making his appeal through us; we entreat you on behalf of Christ, be reconciled to God" (2 Cor. 5:18-20). In countries where CETs are most likely to work, I would argue that there are at least three kinds of reconciliation to which Western Christians are called:

- The first is reconciliation between God and humankind. In many of the countries where CETs work, Christian presence of any kind is relatively weak. Furthermore, many people in these countries may have negative feelings toward Christianity (often due to its Western ties), or at least a strong sense of distance from the Christian faith. There is a sense that Christianity is a religion which belongs to other peoples and cultures. In such countries, an important task of CETs is not only making the Christian faith better understood, but also reducing the negative feelings and sense of "other-ness" which distance local people from God and his love.

- A second important need is for reconciliation between nations. While conflict between people of different nations and cultures is as inevitable as human sin, this is not the condition God desires for humanity and it is the responsibility of CETs, to the extent that it is within their power, to exert themselves to build better understanding and relations between people of different nations and cultures. The call for CETs is not to become apologists for their home countries, but rather to show their love for both their home and host countries by endeavoring to build bridges of understanding and peace between them.

- A final need is for reconciliation between churches of different nations and traditions. Many of the countries where CETs work already have Christian churches and communities, but the ties of fellowship and mutual understanding between these churches and churches of other nations and traditions may be weak. Furthermore, as noted above, past relations with other Christian groups may have left a legacy of grievances which call for healing. Through participating in and learning about the life of the church in their host countries, CETs are in a position not only to enhance mutual understanding between churches in their host and home countries, but also to build better relations between churches which might otherwise have little contact.

This work of reconciliation can be carried out in a variety of ways, but essential to all of them is the quality of CETs' lives and work in the host country. Through work in countries where past sins have sometimes stained the good name of Christ, CETs have the opportunity through their lives and service to help win back the good reputation the name of Christ calls for. Peter Kuzmic writes of how he tells seminary students in Yugoslavia that one of their main tasks in witness is simply to "wash the face of Jesus" in order to help people see past the sins of the church—and also the antagonistic propaganda of its opponents—to the person and love of Christ.[16] In a similar way, I will argue that it is the special mission of CETs, in the name of God, to work to bring down the walls of grievance which often separate people from each other and from the love of God. In particular it is their calling to work for reconciliation between Western Christians and the people—both Christian and non-Christian—of nations which have often associated Christianity more with the power of the West than with the power of God's love. In part this task involves carrying on that which was best in the Western mission effort of the past, namely witness and service in the spirit of love and sacrifice which led many Western missionaries literally to give their lives that more people around the world would come to experience God's love. However, it also involves trying to heal wounds of the past by living out a witness of respect and humility.

Equally essential, I believe, is the need for CETs to be learners as well as teachers. For CETs, learning about the host country, its culture, and its language is not only a way to enhance their ability to function in that culture, but is also in and of itself a form of ministry and witness. It is thus to this issue that we turn next.

3

Learning as Witness

Missionary anthropologist Charles Kraft was once asked how much time a person going abroad for two months as a short-term missionary should spend studying the local language. His answer was: "Two months." When the inquirer asked the same question about a missionary going abroad for six months, Kraft's answer was: "Spend six months in language learning." And when the inquirer asked about a missionary going abroad for two years, Kraft's response was: "There is nothing he could do that would communicate more effectively than spending those two years in language learning. Indeed, if we do no more than engage in the process of language learning we will have communicated more of the essentials of the Gospel than if we devote ourselves to any other task I can think of."[1]

It may seem somewhat odd to begin a discussion of the mission roles of CETs with an entire chapter devoted to the importance of being a learner. After all, the primary business of CETs is teaching, so one could reasonably assume that our discussion should begin with teaching-related issues. However, I have chosen to address it early in this book because the issue of how much time and energy to devote to language and culture study is one that will vex many if not all CETs. Furthermore, while the great majority of CETs want to learn as much as possible of the host language and culture, the obstacles hindering CETs' study of language and culture are considerable, and the result is that CETs are probably *less* likely to learn the host language and culture than other kinds of missionaries are.

Essentially this chapter is a sustained argument that, despite the obstacles CETs face in their efforts to learn the local language and culture, such an attempt is well worth the effort. Study of foreign languages is beneficial for any English teacher in any setting, but it is especially important for CETs because of the many ways that language and culture study enhance their effectiveness in the host culture, both as English teachers and as ambassadors of God's love. It will often not be possible for CETs—especially those who are only in the host country for a year or so—to master the language of their host country or to become experts in its culture. But it is possible and desirable for all CETs to devote a portion of their time to that effort. My hope is that this chapter will encourage as many as possible to do so.

Obstacles to Language Learning

The effort required to learn a new language is considerable for any potential missionary, and the problems CETs face in this regard are by no means unique. However, CETs face a number of special obstacles which eventually discourage many from making more than a token attempt to learn their host country's culture and especially language. Among the main obstacles are the following:

Short stays in the host country: One reason many CETs fail to learn much of the host language or culture is that their stays in the host country are often relatively brief. While some CETs live in their host country for years, the trend in Western mission work has been more and more toward short-term programs and contracts. It is not unusual for CETs to spend only a year or less in the host country. (Many agencies sponsor summer English programs that are only a few weeks long.) Clearly this is not adequate time to gain significant knowledge of a foreign language or culture, especially given that most CETs work in non-Western nations whose languages are very different from English, hence harder to learn. Even CETs who expect to be in the host country a year or two are often discouraged from serious study of the host language by the knowledge that no matter how much effort they invest in learning the new language, they will achieve a passable command of it only as they near the end of their term.

Adequacy of English for work: The daily work of many kinds of missionaries throws them into the local language and culture, and a good knowledge of the host language and culture is often an essential prerequisite to being able to do their jobs. For example, pastors and evangelists need a good command of the host language in order to preach and converse with local people. Similarly, medical and community workers generally have extensive contact with local people who can't speak English, and this means they not only need to know the local language but also have ample opportunity to practice using it. In contrast, CETs can generally conduct their duties adequately without use of the host language (most CETs usually teach in English), so their work actually tends to isolate them from the local language and culture by ensuring that they spend much of their time in a setting where the language medium is English.

Adequacy of English for daily life: CETs often live in towns or cities which are large enough that there are other English speakers nearby, either host nationals who know English or other Westerners. Because English has become the world's most international language, there is a good chance that anyone in the host country who speaks a language other than his or her native tongue will speak English. CETs are also often surrounded by their English students, who often also serve as friends, helpers, and interpreters. Thus, it is generally possible for CETs to get by materially and socially without learning the host language.

Lack of institutional support: Many sending agencies do not require or support the kind of language training for CETs that would be required of most mission personnel. This is more often the case for CETs on short-term contracts than for those on longer terms of service, and many agencies which send CETs abroad for longer terms of service do require study of the host language. However, because it is widely assumed that CETs don't really need foreign language skills for either their work or daily life, even CETs who serve for longer terms are somewhat less likely to be provided with language study opportunities than are other kinds of missionaries. In the absence of full-time language study, CETs who try to learn the host language often have to do so during scraps of free time leftover at the end of the working day.

Expectations of the teacher role: In the minds of both local people and CETs themselves, it is generally assumed that a CET's primary duty is to be a teacher, not a learner, and this expectation can gently undermine a CET's attempts to learn. Because people in the host community view CETs as teachers rather than learners, they may not provide much encouragement or assistance for CETs who wish to learn the host language. In fact, they may sometimes even consider a CETs' efforts to learn the host language an unnecessary diversion of time that could be better spent teaching or providing English practice opportunities for students. The teacher role may also subtly encourage CETs themselves to underestimate the importance of their own efforts to learn.

Previous language learning experiences: To a greater extent than speakers of other languages, many English-speaking Westerners have never learned to speak another language to any real degree of proficiency and thus haven't developed the learning strategies and study habits which make for successful language learning. Such previous experiences as CETs have had with language learning, for example in foreign language courses in high school, generally give them more proficiency in cramming for tests than in actual mastery of a foreign language. When confronted with an utterly alien language for which there may not even be textbooks, CETs may end up overwhelmed. The problem is compounded by unreasonable expectations. It is widely believed that once CETs are living in the host country, they will "pick up" the language (the term "pick up" seems to imply a kind of quick, effortless osmosis). When learning the host language turns out to involve a long period of hard work, it is easy for CETs to become discouraged and quit.

Attitude: A more subtle but serious problem English-speaking Westerners sometimes bring to the problem of language learning is one of attitude. To put it bluntly, the nations of the English-speaking West have for so long led the world that it is almost second nature for Westerners to assume it is natural and right for people of other countries to learn English—and somehow unfair to expect Westerners to go through a commensurate amount of labor to master someone else's language, especially if that language is perceived as "difficult" (i.e., if it is of a language family distant from English, and is written in a different kind of script than English). While few CETs would ever state such a feeling as blatantly as I have above, it often quietly underlies CETs' expectations that people of the host country *should* learn English—and that people of the host country should be understanding if CETs don't learn the local language.

The result of all these obstacles is that it is very easy for CETs' good intentions about learning the host language to remain just that—good intentions—and for CETs' language skills to never progress beyond the basic phrases necessary for survival. For similar reasons, many CETs also never gain more than a superficial understanding of the culture and history of their host country. As understandable as this is, it is also tragic because there are so many important reasons why CETs—even those who only stay in the host country a few months—should learn as much of the host language and culture as possible.

Benefits of Language and Culture Learning

Having examined some of the obstacles which may discourage CETs from attempting to study the host language and culture in any depth, we turn here to the many good reasons why such an investment of time and effort is worthwhile.

Empathy and effectiveness as a language teacher

As Kitty Purgason argues, one of the main benefits of studying the host language is that it enhances CETs' ability to empathize with students and understand what the language learning process looks and feels like from a student perspective.[2] Such study is no doubt valuable even for CETs who are veteran language learners, but is especially important for CETs who have not previously had much language learning experience.

One of the most valuable things CETs can learn from study of the host language is the degree to which a new language can be confusing, overwhelming, and even terrifying. One might assume this point is obvious to CETs, but it often isn't. For English teachers who are native speakers (as most CETs are), English seems wonderfully clear and simple. It is easy to assume that one or two explanations of, for example, the verb tense system should be sufficient to enable students to grasp it. It is often only study of another language that shows (or reminds) CETs how easily one can be confused or overwhelmed by a new language. Needless to say, the exact types of challenges a CET experiences studying the host language may differ considerably from the problems students encounter studying English. For Russian, the problem may be learning the case system; for Japanese, matching forms of words to the appropriate level of politeness; for Chinese, memorizing Chinese characters, and so forth. However, the general experience of confronting whatever challenges the host language offers does much to enhance CETs' ability to feel empathy and compassion for students as CETs shepherd them through the mazes and snares of English. (The role of compassion in language teaching will be discussed further in chapter 5.)

Another benefit of studying the host language is that it helps CETs learn more about methods and strategies for language learning. Ideally, an English teacher's job is not just teaching students English, but also helping them become more effective language learners. Unfortunately, CETs' native knowledge of English does not equip them well for this latter task. There are significant differences between how children in English-speaking environments learn English and how adolescents or adults learn English in environments where English is not often spoken. Granted, there are also similarities between the two processes, but even to the extent that the two processes are similar, CETs' memories of how they learned English are likely to be too dim to be of much use.

Study of other languages gives CETs the opportunity to try out different language learning methods and strategies. The more experience CETs have as language learners, the larger their bag of language learning tricks will be and the more able they will be to assess the effectiveness of a given method for a given situation. Obviously, what worked for a CET in one situation may not work for a student learning English in a different situation, and one of the things a language teacher should teach students is that they each need to discover what works best for them in their situation. However, as a general rule, the more experience CETs have with different language learning strategies, the more effectively they will be able to coach students. Perhaps even more important, the more experience CETs have as language learners, the more they will be aware of the importance of helping students become skilled language learners.

One additional lesson which language learning experience can drive home to CETs is the importance of encouraging students to take the initiative in their own language learning. The view many teachers and students naturally take of the language learning process tends to be rather teacher-focused. It is assumed that if students cooperatively do what the teacher tells them to do, they will eventually learn the target language. However, in order to make much progress in language learning, students generally need to actively take the initiative instead of just doing what they are told. This often means going beyond what the teacher requires, and learning because the student wants to learn instead of because it is required. CETs who spend much time really trying to learn foreign languages usually discover that passively following the teacher's instructions in and of itself often isn't enough to generate real progress in language learning.

Culture shock and preserving a good attitude toward the host culture

One of the most important reasons CETs should make an effort to learn as much as possible of the local language and culture, especially if they will be in the host country for longer periods of time, is that this will help them maintain a more positive attitude toward the host culture and its people. Of course most CETs start out with a good attitude toward their host culture, but within a few months it is not unusual for that enthusiasm to begin to dwindle. Over time some CETs eventually wind up becoming almost hostile toward the people they have come to serve. It is sad when CETs are reduced to complaining frequently about the host country and all the strange things the people there do; in short, when they become missionaries who want to share God's love with the host people, but don't like the host people very much. Often this change in attitude is the result of what is commonly called "culture shock."

Culture shock is a set of adaptation problems which may affect any person who lives in a new culture for a length of time. Often it is described as a feeling of being lost or overwhelmed which people experience when they move to a new and unfamiliar culture. It is also sometimes called "culture fatigue"[3] because life in a new and unfamiliar culture places unusually high demands on a person's reserves of energy, not least because of the strain of constantly communicating in a foreign language or—as is often true for CETs—of having to communicate in simple English with people who do not speak English very well.

The relevance of this culture shock issue for CETs is that a number of its symptoms can have a serious negative impact on CETs' attitudes toward the host culture, hence on the quality of their Christian witness. One problematic result of culture shock is a tendency to withdraw from the host cul-

ture and its people. As CETs become more drained by interaction with the host culture, there is temptation to pull away,
thereby reducing friction and wear. Often the result is that
CETs spend more time with other expatriates, gathering into
little groups of Westerners among whom it is acceptable to
criticize the host country and complain about the difficulties
of trying to live there. In limited quantities, such with-
drawals into a group may be helpful as a break, but the more
CETs withdraw from the host culture, the less likely it is that
they will ever really come to understand the host culture or
be comfortable in it.

Another common result of culture shock is a tendency to
become less patient and more irritable, especially with members of the host culture. This can lead to being increasingly
critical of—or even hostile to—the host culture and its people. During a CETs' early days in the host culture, the new
customs, behaviors, and ideas of the local people seem interesting and perhaps quaint, but as culture fatigue sets in these
same things can become annoying and frustrating. Inability
to understand why people in the host culture behave as they
do can lead to the assumption that host nationals are irra-
tional, backward, or even stupid. Unpleasant encounters
with local people tend to turn into grievances and war stories which are passed around the expatriate community.

While most CETs guard against tendencies to become
hostile toward the host culture at large, what sometimes
happens is that CETs gradually (and often subconsciously)
begin to think of people in the host culture as falling into
"sheep and goats" categories. The sheep are the "good" host
nationals, those who CETs like more and find more reasonable or easier to deal with. These are the people on whom
some CETs come to lavish most of their attention and affection, and with whom they make a serious and generally successful effort to control any feelings of hostility. This group
often consists in large part of students. In contrast, other
host nationals wind up as "goats." Sadly, for some CETs this
group comes to include many members of society at large—
inefficient store clerks, crowds on buses, people who aren't

sufficiently sanitary, and the like. This group is especially likely to include those who are in positions of power, be they government officials or even school staff. By mentally classifying such people as "goats," CETs at times allow themselves to harbor attitudes which they would otherwise realize are inconsistent with Christian charity.

Learning the language and culture of the host culture is one of the best long-term strategies for coping with culture shock, combating negative attitudes toward the host culture, and adapting successfully to life in the host culture. When CETs leave their home environment to go live in a new country and culture, they leave many of the people, things, and activities that provide them with comfort, support, joy, refreshment, and even a sense of purpose—family, friends, social activities, church services, films, books, television, and a host of other things. In large part, the process of adapting to life in a new culture is one of finding new sources of comfort, support, and renewal to replace those left behind. The problem in the host country is not just that everything is new, but that the language and culture barrier restricts the access of CETs to many of the people, activities, and things in the host culture which could potentially serve as new sources of support, comfort, and refreshment. Learning the local language and culture facilitates this process in several ways:

- Most obviously, as CETs gain a better understanding of the host language and culture, they generally experience less stress, wear and tear living in the host culture. To some extent, this comes about just because daily life becomes easier. For example, visiting the market or post office ceases being a test of ability to gesture and may even become a pleasant opportunity for social interaction. Perhaps more important, as CETs gain a better knowledge of what is going on around them, they feel more in control of their environment and the sense of disorientation which contributes so much to culture shock diminishes. When CETs can make sense of what is going on around them and have greater confidence in their ability to predict what others will do and say, they tend to feel more relaxed and at home in the host culture.

- Building personal relationships with people in the host culture is an important part of the process of adapting to life in the host culture—and of counteracting the negative effects of culture shock. Relationships with people of the host culture give CETs a positive emotional tie to the culture which often more than compensates for difficulties they encounter in adjusting. It also means CETs will have more friends and emotional support. Studies show that sojourners (people who go to live in a new culture) who are able to make friends in the host culture are generally more successful in adjusting well to life in the host country. Often it is with the making of the first friendship that a sojourner begins to feel more at home in the host culture.[4] As CETs gain some degree of skill in the local language, they can interact with a much greater number of people in the host culture, hence a much larger pool of potential friends and acquaintances. (In contrast, CETs who only speak English are restricted not only to a much narrower circle of people within the host culture, but also often to social interaction in less-than-perfect English.)
- CETs who speak the local language have access to a much broader range of the host country's culture products such as books, newspapers, television, and films. This opens up many new avenues for better understanding of the host culture and helps CETs appreciate the depth and richness of the host culture in ways that are difficult or impossible when restricted to information available in English.

Consider how people often react to hearing people talking in an unfamiliar language. To someone overhearing a conversation in a language he or she doesn't speak, it sounds like a series of meaningless babbling noises, like the chattering of monkeys (hence the universal temptation to mimic speakers of unfamiliar languages by making gibberish noises). No matter how sophisticated the conversation actually is, the outsider is totally unable to appreciate it. Likewise, CETs who view the host culture from the outside are likely to have at best a superficial understanding of it, missing much of its sophistication and richness. Naturally CETs who only experience the host culture as a cacophony of quaint people interacting through a series of funny-sounding noises will be tempted to feel that their own culture is more mature. Even when CETs are cognitively aware that there is much more to the host culture than they can understand, their inability to actually see and appreciate these riches makes this belief an abstract statement of faith based in theory rather than a powerful concrete experience. In contrast, CETs who can speak the host language will be able to gain a more tangible and genuine appreciation of the culture's complexity and meaning. This, in turn, helps CETs develop and maintain both interest in and respect for the host culture.

The issue of culture shock is one CETs need to take seriously because they will not be very effective as God's emissaries if they lose their love for the people they serve (cf. 1 Cor. 13:1-3). In the long run the most effective antidote to culture shock lies in becoming more at home in the host culture, and in gaining a better understanding of the host language and culture.[5]

"Translating" the gospel

"Translating" the gospel refers here not to the work of Bible translation, but rather to the process by which Christianity is inculturated into a new culture, becoming an integral part of that culture rather than an alien faith.[6] For CETs to be a constructive part of this process, it helps greatly if they can speak the local language and understand the local culture so that they can both live out and talk about the Christian faith in ways that make it seem as much a part of the local culture as possible.

From the very beginning, the gospel has always come to people in the context of a specific culture. The primary example of this is the incarnation of Jesus Christ himself, who came to earth in a particular place and time to live and teach in a particular cultural context, and stated his message in the idiom of the Jewish people among whom he lived. As Lesslie Newbigin points out, it is impossible to have a version of the gospel which is "unadulterated by cultural accretions." The Word is the word made flesh, and "[T]here can never be a culture-free gospel."[7] However, God's message was not long confined to the Jewish community and was soon "translated" into Greek culture (both figuratively and literally in the sense of Bible translation) and then eventually into the Latin culture and language, thus beginning a process by which the gospel has become incarnate in hundreds of human cultures and languages.

Lamin Sanneh makes the compelling argument that one of the main reasons Christianity has become the world's most truly international faith lies in the way it is able to reach across cultural lines and become "translated" into new cultures. Sanneh notes: "Translatability is the source of the success of Christianity across cultures. The religion is the willing adoption of any culture that would receive it, equally at home in all languages and cultures, and among all races and conditions of people." Although in all cultures the gospel serves a standard against which Christians must measure cultural practices, the gospel can be adopted and contextualized into any culture, and it is possible for people anywhere in the world to become Christians without abandoning their culture.[9]

In many of the cultures to which CETs go, the process of "translating" the gospel has already begun and may be well underway. In some of these countries, there are ancient Christian churches which have centuries of experience interacting with the local culture.[10] Others have Christian churches which were founded decades or centuries ago by Western missionaries, and which also have a rich fund of experience in the task of making the gospel relevant to the local culture. CETs will be more effective as ambassadors for the gospel in their host culture if they draw on the work and insights of previous Christians—local Christians and missionaries—who have already devoted much effort to the task of bringing the gospel to life in the local culture. As Paul Hiebert notes: "Cross cultural translation and communication are no easy tasks. If we do not understand this, we are in danger of being ineffective messengers at best, and at worst of communicating a gospel that is misunderstood and distorted."[11]

The danger for CETs who know little about their host culture, and about how the gospel has already become contextualized within that culture, is that their overall impact may be more to disseminate a Western version of Christianity rather than to facilitate its translation into the local culture. In part this is because CETs' work as teachers of Western language and culture creates a natural pull toward viewing and talking about Christianity in a Western context. For example, CETs who want an opportunity to present the Christian faith in the classroom often justify it on the grounds that it is an important part of Western culture, and then tend to stress those aspects of Christianity most closely identified with Western culture, such as customs for celebrating Christmas and Easter. While God can no doubt bless and work with the efforts of CETs who disseminate a Western version of Christianity, such an approach seems to be at odds with the genius of God's desire for Christianity to incarnate itself anew in each culture.

If CETs are to be effective translators of the gospel in the host culture, they need to learn as much as possible about the local culture. In other words, they need to learn to see and understand the world as people in the host culture do, because it is through these perceptual lenses that the local people will view the Christian faith and judge the behavior of CETs. The more CETs are able to talk about the gospel in ways that make sense to people in the host culture, and to live it out in ways appropriate to the local culture, the more CETs will be able to proclaim and live out a witness that brings the Christian faith closer to the host culture and its people (cf. 1 Cor. 9:19-22).[12]

Reconciliation through building relationships

A final benefit of CETs' efforts to learn the language and culture of their host country is that such efforts provide an opportunity to build relationships with local people. Moreover, by placing the CET in the relatively humble posture of a learner, this approach to building relationships demonstrates CETs' respect and even love for host people. Consequently it helps further the process of reconciliation between people of the host country and the West, and also ultimately between humankind and God.

Building relationships of the teacher-student variety is not difficult for CETs in most settings. In fact, it is not uncommon for CETs to discover after several months in the host country that their social community consists overwhelmingly of their students. Given the difference in role and often age between CETs and students, this may seem a little odd; however, on reflection the reasons for this are fairly obvious. In many host countries, students are the host nationals with whom CETs have most regular contact, hence the people CETs most naturally come to know. Also, in colleges or boarding schools, students are transients and relative newcomers in the school community, and it tends to be easier for a newly arrived CET to make friends with other newcomers than with established long-term residents of the community.[13]

It is clearly desirable for CETs to have good relationships with their students, but relying on students as their primary friendship group can also be problematic for CETs because it may be difficult for a CET to balance the roles of teacher and friend without creating the appearance of favoritism toward students with whom a CET is especially close. Students may also find the mixed teacher/friend role new and confusing, and may see friendship as a sign of favoritism—and permission to act as specially privileged favorites. The potential for confusion and problems is increased by the fact that CETs and students may have very differing cultural notions as to what norms are appropriate for student-teacher relationships, and this may lead to misunderstanding as students and CETs misinterpret each others' signals and intentions.

It would seem more natural for CETs to find their primary social community among other staff and teachers at the host school, but this is often easier said than done. Some CETs will be fortunate enough to have colleagues who take the initiative in integrating CETs into their community. But it may also be the case, especially in schools where there have been previous foreign teachers, that colleagues will not take much initiative to get to know CETs. One reason for this lies in the transient nature of many CET teaching positions. Colleagues may have taken the initiative to get to know previous foreign teachers, only to have those teachers disappear from their lives after a year or two, and after this happens once or twice local teachers' enthusiasm for developing relationships with CETs may dampen. Many Westerners, North Americans in particular, are accustomed to a transient society in which people easily make and leave friends, but in most cultures friendships are made more slowly and invested with more significance. After having one relationship with a Westerner uprooted, people in many cultures become less eager to go through the process again.

Another reason local teachers are sometimes reluctant to reach out to foreign colleagues lies in their English skills. Some local English teachers speak English fluently and confidently, but in many countries it is not unusual for local teachers to be more proficient in grammar, vocabulary, and reading than in speaking and listening. In situations where English is taught but never used, the weakness of their oral skills is not obvious. However, when local teachers need to interact with a Westerner in English their lack of oral skills is painfully exposed, and desire to avoid this pain may make local English teachers reluctant to interact with Western English teachers. (This is especially true in Asia where maintaining "face" is an important cultural imperative.)

For these reasons, CETs often need to be both active and creative in seeking out ways to build relationships with colleagues, not to mention other host nationals in the community. Part of this art of building relationships lies in finding ways to reach out to local people that local people will find natural and comfortable. This is where CETs' efforts to learn the local language and culture come in. One of the most natural reasons for reaching out to people in the host culture lies in CETs' need to learn the host language and culture. This is a need local people will readily understand. It will generally seem quite natural that a CET would approach them for help with the local language or to ask about the local culture. Furthermore, local people will often take joy and pride in explaining their language and culture to an interested CET.

This strategy of using CETs' need to learn local language and culture as a vehicle for building relationships can take a variety of forms. Perhaps the most obvious is for CETs to formally recruit teachers or tutors who will teach CETs the local language or some aspect of the local culture. Regardless of how much progress CETs make in their study, it provides sustained contact with a teacher or tutor and allows CETs to get to know at least one member of the local community at a deeper level. (This is by no means a new idea—historically many missionaries' first friends in the community have been the teachers with whom they study the local language.)

However, the learning strategy should be broadened beyond the one or two local people who a CET might engage as a regular teacher. Ideally, CETs should view all people in the host country as potential teachers. For example, CETs can approach colleagues with questions about the host school, the curriculum, students, and the educational system of the host country. Students can be approached with questions about local culture and history. Even neighbors and local shopkeepers can be approached with questions about how to say things in the local language.

This strategy of using CETs' need to learn as an occasion for building relationships has the great advantage of placing local people in the roles of expert and teacher, and of placing CETs in the relatively humble student role. This is important because, as noted in chapter 2, one unfortunate legacy of the West's past and present relations with the rest of the world is a widespread impression that the people of the West—especially Americans—consider themselves to be superior to people of other nations and cultures. As Richard

Payne writes: "Many third world elites view most Americans as a people who assume that they are racially and culturally superior, who are ignorant and disdainful of other civilizations, and who are eager to teach but disinclined to learn from others."[14] If the teacher role is the only one CETs play in the host community, this impression may inadvertently be reinforced. (Granted, this impression is to some extent unavoidable. After all, there is no getting around the fact that CETs are teachers. Also, the need of people in the host country to learn the language of the West suggests that the West has much to offer.)

In this context it makes a significant difference when CETs turn a one-sided process into a genuine exchange, one which consists not just of people from the host culture learning the preeminent language of the West, but rather of CETs and people in the host culture each learning each other's languages and cultures. By choosing to study the host language and culture, CETs dramatically change the nature of their relationship with the host community, and suggest in a powerful way that the people of the host country have just as much to teach as they do to learn. By taking on a humble learner posture, CETs can "give face" to the host culture and its people, and also work toward reconciliation by helping heal one of the particularly painful wounds of the past.[15]

Understanding of the host language and culture is not easy for CETs to achieve. It is only purchased at a price that includes the sacrifice of considerable time and effort. However, it is the very cost of this effort that makes language and culture study such convincing evidence of a CETs' interest in, respect for, and even love of the host culture and its people. There are also other powerful ways by which CETs can demonstrate their love, not least being the very fact that CETs choose to live with and serve the people of their host country. However, affirmations of respect that are supported by sincere efforts to learn the local language and culture are especially convincing. Significantly, when God showed his love for the world in the incarnation, he did more than come to live in the world and be with humankind. He also paid a price for that love that left no question of its authenticity. In a small way, study of the host language and culture can similarly serve as one way to demonstrate CETs' love for their host country and its people.

Learning the Host Language and Culture

The issue of how to learn languages and cultures is worthy of far more discussion than is possible here, and I would refer the reader to a number of excellent book-length treatments of the issue.[16] Here I will confine myself to a few general observations as to what constitute reasonable goals.

It would be unrealistic to expect that all CETs should become fluent in the language of their host country, if for no other reason than that many CETs do not live in the host country long enough to make such a goal practicable. Even CETs who live in the host country for several years or more need to balance the need to spend time on language learning with the need to attend to their teaching duties. It takes a considerable investment of time to learn any foreign language, and many of the host languages CETs need to learn are more difficult and time-consuming to learn than languages such as Spanish, French, or German that are more closely related to English. CETs are thus often faced with the difficult choice of devoting a significant amount of time to language learning—time that has to be taken away from other activities—or accepting a lower level of achievement in the host language.

My feeling is that despite the time and effort involved, CETs who plan to be in the host country for several years or more should strive to gain a good conversational knowledge of the host language, and ideally also at least basic literacy. This may require a year or so of full-time study either before the CET begins working in the host country or after the CET has worked there long enough to know that he or she is committed to a longer term of service. It will also generally require the CET to find time for daily study and practice of the host language even after the completion of full-time language study. In particular, after CETs develop reading skills, they need to go on and apply these skills to the task. The benefits of literacy in the host language are not reaped in full unless a CET develops the habit of reading books, magazines, newspapers, and so forth in the host language.

Expectations for CETs who will only live in the host country for a year or so, or perhaps even only a few months or weeks, are necessarily lower, but this does not mean that short-term CETs should ignore the issue of language learning entirely. Some of the advantages of learning the host language mentioned above accrue mainly to those who achieve a relatively high level of skill in the language. However, other benefits begin to accrue right from the start, the most important of these being the message of respect that language study sends. Even early faltering attempts to speak a little of the host language are a strong signal to the host community of a CETs' interest in the host community. In fact, the very fact that these early efforts to speak are difficult suggests that the CET is interested enough to undergo a degree of discomfort and even embarrassment in order to make the attempt.

What I would suggest for short-term CETs, or even for longer-term CETs who do not expect to ever achieve fluency in the host language, is a minimal but sustained attempt to keep learning a little more of the host language. What is most important here is not that CETs progress rapidly, or that they achieve a high level of fluency, but rather that they not let their interest in the host language die. There are dangers in this approach, the main one being that slow progress tends to be discouraging. Learners who feel they are not making progress are prone to giving up. However, if a CET can maintain enough discipline to study a little every week and perhaps meet with a tutor once a week, this slow-but-steady approach will result in progress. Equally important it will help keep the CET reminded of the importance of continuing to make the effort to reach out to local people on their own terms. In order to achieve this goal, it is not necessary that CETs ever become fluent, it is only necessary that they keep trying.

With regard to study of the host culture, the primary goal is—to the extent possible—to learn to see the world as the people of the host culture do, learning how they understand themselves and also how they view other peoples and cultures. It is especially important to make an effort to develop an empathetic view of the "hard" parts of the culture, i.e., those beliefs, attitudes, customs, values, and behaviors which are most difficult for Westerners and Western Christians to accept and deal with. Examples of such might include prejudicial attitudes toward women, lack of concern toward the plight of the poor, minimal attention to safety, or prejudice against minorities or foreigners. (Obviously many of these problems can be found in Western cultures as well.) Often an important part of coming to terms with these more difficult aspects of the host culture is gaining a good understanding of the culture's "story," the history which reflects a people's sense of identity and place in the world. While CETs may not fully accept all of these ways of thinking and acting, they at least need to understand why people in the host culture think and act as they do. Understanding this story is especially important to CETs because attitudes which people in the host culture have toward outsiders, Westerners, and Christians were usually shaped by events of the past. Understanding why members of the host culture think, act, and feel as they do not only enhances understanding of the culture in general, hence ability to fairly represent it to others, but also makes these difficult aspects of the culture somewhat easier to accept or at least live with.

Conclusion

Reconciliation is something to be lived out as much as preached. We see this most clearly in the life of Jesus, a life that was devoted to living among people, caring for them, and serving them as much as it was to reaching them with words. Jesus Christ not only preached reconciliation; he brought it about by becoming a human being and ultimately giving himself as a sacrifice to bring about reconciliation between humankind and God. Perhaps the greatest miracle of history is recorded in Philippians (2:5-8): "Jesus Christ, who, though he was in the form of God, did not regard equality with God as something to be exploited, but emptied himself, taking the form of a slave, being born in human likeness. And being found in human form, he humbled himself and became obedient to the point of death—even death on a cross."

As ambassadors of the church, one important task of CETs is to live among the people they serve in a way that will build toward reconciliation between Western Christians and people of different cultures, and also between humankind and God. If Christ's example is taken as an indication of how this task is to be accomplished, it will involve becoming as closely integrated as possible into the communities they serve, and also approaching the people they live among from a humble position of servanthood. This requires being learners as well as teachers.

Studying the language and culture of the host country doesn't just prepare CETs for witness and service in that country. In and of itself it is a vitally important part of that witness, not least because of the message of respect which such efforts send. If CETs' entire life in the host culture is devoted to teaching their own language and culture, it is hard to escape creating the impression that this is all they consider worthwhile. In contrast, if CETs find the time to place themselves in the learner role, they automatically elevate those around them to the teacher role, and there is no better way to demonstrate that they value and respect those around them.

4

English Teaching as Witness

Many Christians who choose to teach English abroad do so in large part out of a desire to bear witness to the good news of Jesus Christ. However, the majority of CETs teach in secular institutions which do not take proclamation of the Christian gospel as part of their agenda. In fact, most CETs work for employers who definitely don't want the Christian faith promoted in class, or perhaps even outside. CETs are consequently faced with the problem of how to bear witness through a secular profession in a setting which does not encourage—or may even desire to prevent—such witness.

While this chapter will make passing mention of evangelistic approaches used by CETs in appropriate settings, I will assume that for most CETs the classroom is less a forum for talking with students about Christianity than a place to show them what Christianity is like in action. My basic position will be that the quality with which CETs carry out their teaching work is a vitally important part of their Christian witness. This idea is illustrated by a story Tom Scovel tells about a member of John Calvin's 16th-century church in Geneva, Switzerland:

> "Calvin was a strong believer in practical and living theology, and he encouraged his parishioners to apply Christianity to every aspect of their daily life. One day, a stranger entered a shoemaker's shop run by one of Calvin's congregation. When the stranger found

English Teaching as Witness / 65

out that the shoemaker was a Christian, he said, somewhat sarcastically, "Oh, well then you must make *Christian* shoes!" "No," the shoemaker quietly replied, "I don't make Christian shoes, but I make shoes well."[1]

Rather than being incidental to witness or even evangelism, the quality of CETs' teaching work is the primary vehicle through which they share the love of God with their students, and also the strongest and clearest statement they make about what a Christian should be like.

This chapter will address the issue of how CETs can live out God's love through the quality of their teaching work. We will also look at how CETs can bear witness through the ways in which they deal with a number of difficult problems raised by their dual nature as teachers of English and ambassadors of the Christian faith, particularly in places where local authorities would not look favorably on the Christian side of a CET's agenda. Finally, given the fact that it is often more obvious to local people that a CET is a Westerner than a Christian, we will look at the question of how CETs publicly identify themselves as Christians.

Christian Witness in the Classroom

Some CETs work in settings where there would seem to be little difficulty combining English teaching with Christian witness and even direct evangelism. Examples of such settings would include Christian schools or church-sponsored English classes in which proclamation of the Christian gospel is an openly stated goal of the educational program and lessons based on Bible texts or Christian faith issues are an accepted part of the curriculum.[2] Other CETs teach in secular settings where promotion of Christian faith is not part of the school's agenda, but where there are also few restrictions on Christian outreach outside of class through activities such as Bible studies, Christian English clubs or camps, or simply through informal conversation and sharing on a one-to-one basis.[3] However, a great many CETs work in settings where evangelism in or even out of class is discouraged by their host institution, government, or society. Many CETs work in settings where evangelism is prohibited outright. For CETs in such settings, the question of how to integrate Christian witness and their teaching work is more obviously a problem.

I would argue that, for CETs in any setting—whether one that allows direct Christian outreach or one in which overt evangelism is prohibited—it would be a great loss if CETs were to limit their understanding of Christian witness to direct and explicit forms of Christian outreach. Rather, as suggested above, CETs should view the quality of their teaching work as the primary means through which they bear witness to God and share his love with students. One reason for this line of reasoning is that, from the perspective of a student of English, the most immediate and pressing need is for assistance in learning English. The best way to demonstrate love to such students is by offering them the help that they need and call for. The diligence with which CETs offer this assistance thus becomes a visible and credible measure of their level of concern for students. (This issue will be addressed further in chapter 5.)

A second reason quality in teaching is such an important aspect of witness is that it reflects directly on the nature of those who follow Christ, and at least indirectly speaks to the nature of God himself. It is primarily in the classroom that CETs will either succeed or fail in developing credibility as individuals. If they are known to be Christians, the quality of their teaching work will also reflect either favorably or unfavorably on Christians as a whole. This is true of teachers in any setting because of the degree to which they live out their working lives in the public spotlight, closely observed by a large and often rather demanding audience. However, it is particularly true of CETs because as foreigners they often attract considerable attention in their host communities. For better or worse, CETs are often very much lamps on a stand and cities on a hill. We must not underestimate the positive Christian witness which CETs can have in class through doing their work responsibly and well.

It is probably neither possible nor necessary to list definitively all the characteristics that constitute quality in an English teacher, but several deserve special note:

Professionalism: Here I refer not to the outer trappings of the professional image—proper attire and the like—but rather a seriousness of purpose, a desire to do one's work well that is backed up by efforts to continually learn and improve. This is particularly important for the many CETs who have limited professional training and experience as language teachers. As noted in chapter 2, many CETs are able to procure teaching positions because they are native speakers of English rather than because they are English teachers by profession. As a result, many Christian English teachers are engaged in jobs for which they have minimal preparation. What makes this situation particularly dangerous is the widespread and pernicious belief that anyone who can speak a language can teach it, a belief which may discourage some CETs from making serious efforts to learn the craft of language teaching. It is true that native speakers of English who are given a minimum of training are often reasonably effective teaching certain kinds of courses, particularly conversation practice courses. However, there is much more to language teaching than being able to start a conversation and a CET new to the profession should constantly strive to learn as much as possible about it.[4]

Even for CETs who have training in language teaching, there are always many things to learn in a new country and educational setting. A CET newly arrived in the host institution will generally be unfamiliar with its teaching materials, curriculum, testing and evaluation systems, and administrative system. The teaching practices and goals of the program will probably also differ to some degree from what the CET is accustomed to, as will the beliefs and customs students have with regard to language learning. For trained CETs, "professionalism" means becoming as familiar as possible with the new setting.

Diligence: Teachers often assess their self-worth and success as teachers on the basis of either how much they are liked by students or their students' levels of achievement. However, no matter how good teachers are, it is not possible to ensure that they will always be popular with students. Both teachers and students have distinct personalities and styles, and the chemistry that results when these styles encounter each other is beyond anyone's ability to control. Likewise, it is not possible for CETs to ensure that they will generally be successful in their attempts to teach English. Students often study English more because they are required to than because they have any genuine interest in the subject, and there are many settings where students are justified in assuming that their best interests are served by minimizing the time they spend on English and maximizing time spent on other classes or on other pursuits.

What CETs do have the power to control is the degree of effort they invest in their work, and in cultures the world over, diligence is generally regarded as one of the cardinal virtues of the teaching profession. Diligence is a fairer measure of whether a CET is a good teacher than popularity or success. Teachers who prepare thoroughly, make a good effort in class, deal with assignments promptly and responsibly, and go the extra mile by giving extra help where it is needed are generally well regarded by both colleagues and students even when they do not come out first in popularity polls or produce the highest test scores.

Concern: On the whole it is no doubt generally best if CETs make an attempt to be friendly with students, and are as nice as possible in class. However, not all CETs are naturally cheerful, outgoing, and friendly, and for many it may be neither natural nor possible to constantly wear a smile in class. What is ultimately more important is that CETs be genuinely concerned with their students' well being, both academically and in general, and also, that they make a serious effort to understand students and meet their needs (see chapter 5). Sometimes what students need is a smile or a kind word of encouragement, other times they need to be challenged, and on yet other occasions what they really need is a word of rebuke or a sound scolding.

Concern for others does not come any more naturally to Christians than it does to anyone else. If the Christian understanding of human nature is correct, our natural impulses run more toward focus on our own needs and well being than toward concern (love) for others, and this does not change just because a person becomes a Christian. By way of reference, note that in Romans 7:14-25 there is little evidence in Paul's vivid description of his struggle with his sinful nature that this struggle has ceased. Concern for students is frequently a matter of consciously deciding to reach out to better understand or help, rather than following natural impulses. In the face of students who are still making the same mistake after the third explanation, love often has more to do with self-control than warm feelings.

Cooperation with colleagues: Many CETs teach in a school or institutional setting and are therefore part of a team and a program. In such settings, it is important for CETs to remember that their Christian witness is not only evident to students, but is also on display in front of their colleagues and superiors. As noted in the previous chapter, CETs sometimes develop a compartmentalized view of the host culture, taking students as the primary audience for their witness and viewing school officials and even colleagues more as obstacles. It is therefore very important that CETs make a conscious attempt to work in cooperation with other school staff, learning about the program and customs of the school community, and working as much as possible in harmony with other members of the team. This will help ensure that the CETs' witness will be a positive one to the host community as a whole, not just to one segment of that community.

The above list of virtues for CETs to aspire to in teaching is hardly exhaustive. In fact, a complete inventory would at minimum require discussion of all of the virtues Paul includes in his list of the fruits of the Spirit: love, joy, peace, patience, kindness, generosity, faithfulness, gentleness, and self-control (Gal. 5:22-23).[5] Suffice it to say that CETs' diligence and professionalism, and their concern for students and colleagues, are important aspects of their role as ambassadors of God. The quality of teaching work done by CETs is in and of itself a powerful recommendation for the Christian faith, and is also the most concrete and immediate way in which CETs incarnate God's love.[6]

Issues Raised by CETs' Dual Role

Christian witness is not simply a matter of how responsibly CETs carry out their work as classroom teachers. It is also a matter of how they deal with a number of issues raised by their dual role as English teachers and ambassadors of the Christian faith. Below we will look at three problems CETs frequently encounter and consider how CETs can deal with each in ways that enhance their Christian witness.

Agendas and integrity

In settings such as church-sponsored English clubs, where it is clear to students that the goal of lessons is to present the Christian message as much as it is to teach English, no ethical issue is raised by a teacher pursuing both English teaching and Christian agendas in class. However, the stated agenda of most English classes is the teaching of English, and whenever a gap develops between this stated agenda and a second unstated Christian agenda being pursued by a CET, the issue of integrity becomes problematic. The problem is most obvious when a CET's true agenda is almost totally at odds with the stated purposes of a class; for example, when a CET uses the English class as a front for evangelistic work and has little genuine interest in teaching English per se. As Kitty Purgason argues: "To preach to a captive audience who came expecting something else is unethical."[7] When students are paying for such a class, a good argument could be made that this is actually fraud.

However, such glaring gaps between the stated purposes and actual intent of CETs' classes are not common. More perplexing are borderline situations where a CET takes a job with every intent of being a responsible English teacher but also has a secondary agenda that is more or less hidden from the employers. As noted earlier, one of the reasons for growth in the number of English teachers sponsored by churches and para-church organizations is that Christian English teachers are welcome in places where evangelistic Christian missionaries would not be. Many nations that desperately need the expertise of native English speakers are not wealthy enough to offer pay packages and living conditions that are internationally competitive, so they are forced to rely heavily on foreign teachers who are willing to work under volunteer terms. There are, of course, many secular organizations that supply such volunteers, but a large portion of the potential volunteer market is made up of Christians whose faith calls them to Christian service and witness even in situations where they must make a sacrifice in terms of salaries and living conditions. The demand for English is such that nations in which Christianity is opposed are often willing to tolerate and even welcome Christian teachers of English despite their Christian faith.

However, in these settings it is generally assumed by governments, institutions, and students that CETs come to the host country as English teachers, not as missionary evangelists. In fact, in some countries CETs are hired only with the explicit provision that they do not evangelize. An issue that CETs need to consider in such settings is: Where does one cross the line between discretion and deception when taking a teaching job with the intent of also engaging in evangelism? A second, related question is: When—if ever—does the imperative to proclaim the gospel override the imperative to be honest and forthright?

These are not easy questions and I have no easy answers. In such situations CETs need to work out God's call with considerable thought and prayer. On the whole, however, I would suggest that the more CETs mislead others as to their true intentions in accepting a teaching position, the more their integrity is compromised and the luster of their witness tarnished. CETs need to take this price into account as they consider the roles to which God calls them in their work.

I do not mean to imply that on job applications Christian

teachers are morally obligated to state that they hold Christian convictions and hope to share those with others. After all, no such standard is normally required of teachers who hold to other worldviews. However, neither should Christians casually assume that the imperative to proclaim the gospel justifies deceptive practices. Whenever people begin to sense that a CET's real reasons for being in the host country are not the reasons stated, Christian witness pays a price in diminished credibility and integrity. Perhaps people in the host country will choose to forgive a CET's lack of forthrightness, especially in countries where they themselves are often unable to be forthright. But Western Christians cannot blithely assume such forgiveness in every place where the church and the gospel meet opposition or are forced to exist within limits. CETs must also take seriously the potential impact that deceptive practices can have on their own spiritual and moral lives—deception too easily becomes a habit.

An additional implication of this issue for CETs is that they should be as transparent as possible in their portrayal of themselves and their goals. This would suggest that even in countries where Christian missionaries are not very welcome, it is best if CETs' Christian faith is known to students, school staff, and the general community—at least to the degree that nobody could ever accuse CETs of trying to conceal it. Here Christ's analogy of the lamp seems particularly relevant; it lights the house much better placed on a stand than hidden under a bushel (Matt. 5:16). There is great room for flexibility as to when and how CETs should let others know about their Christian faith, but when they are too careful and discreet about telling people that they are Christian, discretion may lead to the impression that they are hiding something.

A final implication of the integrity issue is that when CETs accept jobs as English teachers, their first agenda must be the effective teaching of English. In fact, as suggested above, it is often through the responsibility with which they carry out their teaching work that their most effective Christian witness is presented. In some countries CETs' openness about their faith may result in their becoming objects of an uncomfortable degree of scrutiny. In others it may even result in hostility. However, such apparent obstacles may work to the advantage of the gospel. In countries where Christian foreigners are the object of suspicion, special attention may well be focused on the way in which they conduct their work, thus the faithfulness with which they carry out their assigned tasks will be more readily noticed.

Ambassador of the West versus ambassador of Christianity

CETs who wish to present a Christian witness in class often attempt to get around restrictions by using lessons on Western culture as an excuse to introduce aspects of the Christian gospel. This is especially common among CETs who teach in countries where proclamation of Christianity is forbidden or where Western Christians are not permitted to be involved in evangelistic activities. In these settings CETs often wait for Christian holidays like Christmas and Easter, and then present lessons on Western holidays that also contain elements of the gospel message. In this way, CETs can justify the discussion of Christianity in class by saying that it is an important aspect of Western culture, hence a necessary and legitimate part of teaching a Western language. While such opportunities to talk about Christianity in class are obviously limited, they play a significant role in many CETs' understanding of what makes their teaching role distinctively Christian. This is also part of how they explain their ministry to Christians back home.

This practice gets around one problem, but only at the risk of creating another. The problem with justifying the introduction of Christianity in class by arguing that it is a part of Western culture is that unless CETs are careful they may create or reinforce the unfortunate impression that Christianity and Western culture are inherently linked. As pointed out in chapter 2, the identification of Christianity with Western culture has been a major obstacle to the spread of the gospel in many countries. Sometimes this was because Christianity came to be identified as the religion of enemy powers, or sometimes just because it came to be identified as foreign—somebody else's religion. In many countries, it is only after Christianity has become less identified with a particular colonial power or with the West in general that it has begun to take root and grow. Thus, by reemphasizing the link between Christianity and Western culture CETs may be strengthening a belief that, in many countries, is one of the most effective obstacles to the Christian faith.

CETs cannot and should not avoid pointing out the important role that Christianity has played in shaping Western culture and history, nor should they play down the importance that it still has in many Western countries. It is a historical fact that Christianity has had enormous influence on the West, and no responsible introduction to the culture of English-speaking nations could ignore Christianity. However, in courses on Western culture CETs need to be careful not to give the mistaken impression that Christianity is inherently a Western religion, or that the West is Christian. Historically, of course, Christianity is not simply a Western religion. It was born in the Middle East rather than Europe, and it arose from a Middle Eastern culture that was decidedly not Western in any contemporary sense of the term. Also, belief in Christianity has never been confined to the West. Some of the world's oldest churches are in distinctly non-Western countries such as Egypt, Ethiopia, and India. And over the last century Christianity has become less and less Western as the church grows in non-Western nations while it weakens in the West, especially Western Europe.

Additionally, the idea that any nation has ever been a Christian nation is at best problematic. While Christianity has been an influential force in the history of many Western nations, there is little evidence that any nation has ever determined national policy primarily on the basis of Christian teaching (especially such teachings as love for one's enemies). The Christian faith stands in critical tension with the cultures of the West just as it does with cultures elsewhere in the world. The notion that Western cultures are somehow more Christian than other cultures is highly problematic at best.[8]

In the course of their work as English teachers, CETs will almost certainly teach about various aspects of Western culture, and they should recognize and even teach about the important role that Christianity has played in shaping Western culture. However, as CETs have occasion to discuss Christianity, they should also make it clear that the Western chapter of the history of Christianity is only one part of the story and that the Christian faith has always been and still continues to be a part of the lives of many outside the West. To the extent that CETs are able to convey this message, they can help put to rest a misunderstanding that often makes people in many cultures feel unnecessarily distant from the good news of God's work in Jesus Christ.

Furthermore, while CETs play a dual role as ambassadors of both Western cultures and the Christian faith, it is also desirable for CETs' Christian witness that people be able to see a distinction in them between these two roles. In other words, it should be clear from what CETs say and do that they do not consider being Westerners and Christians part of the same package. To this end, as CETs have occasion to talk about what Westerners and Christians might feel or believe, it is important that they make a distinction between the two groups, recognizing that while there is overlap between the two groups, they are most definitely not identical. CETs need to keep in mind that they represent two rather different "we's," one being "we Westerners" and one "we Christians." To the extent that people in the host country hear and see the distinction between these two identities in a CET, they are less likely to assume that the two are one and the same.

Evangelism and the power of the teacher

One of the most basic realities of classrooms is that teachers virtually always have authority and power over their students. The degree of this power varies greatly from one situation to the next. In a school setting where the grades a teacher issues may determine a student's future, the degree of power is considerable. In an informal evening conversation class for adults, the teacher's power may be considerably less. However, even in the latter setting, it would be naïve to assume that the teacher does not exert any power at all. In most cultures the role of teacher inherently carries with it a degree of power and influence, even when no grading is involved. Also, the fact that English is a scarce and precious commodity, and that foreign teachers are even rarer, gives CETs an added degree of power and influence.

The question we must ask ourselves is what impact unequal power relationships have on attempts to promote the gospel. We might pause to consider the fact that in the incarnation God chose to become part of the human race not at a position of influence and social standing, but rather among its lower ranks. It was from this lowly position that Jesus then preached the gospel, relying not on earthly authority to gain himself a hearing, but on the authority inherent in the truth of what he preached. Those Jesus chose as disciples and followers were poor people of low social standing, yet it was to such people that Jesus entrusted the proclamation of the gospel after his resurrection. It was on such people that he built the nucleus of his church. Of course there are cases in the biblical record of Jesus' followers using earthly privilege to promote God's kingdom—Paul's career provides several examples of this. However, even Paul's tendency is to revel in his weakness (as in 1 Cor. 1:27 and 2 Cor. 12:10) rather than relying on his social role or standing to carry the gospel forward. God's way seems to be one of offering the gospel to people rather than relying on worldly power to force them to accept it.

My concern here is not that CETs will knowingly use their power as teachers to coerce students toward a profession of faith. The unjustness of such behavior would obviously generate resentment and severely tarnish any positive witness a CET might hope to have. The greater danger lies in CETs being insufficiently aware of how the power inherent in their roles affects the way students respond to their interest in proclaiming the gospel, whether in or outside class. In one such scenario, students gradually discover that the CET is very interested in sharing his or her faith, and tends to be quite pleased when he or she has a chance to do so. This gently tempts students to express an interest in Christianity in order to get on the teacher's better side and get what they want (better grades, more chances to practice English, whatever). A closely related scenario arises from the fact that students often serve as CETs' primary social community. Those students who become a CET's friends often also become the most natural people with whom a CET can share his or her faith. This places students who have found special favor with the CET in a position where they feel greater pressure to respond positively—or at least politely—to the gospel, lest their special standing as the teacher's friend be endangered. In a final scenario, students respond positively to a CET's attempts to share the gospel more out of a culturally bound desire to please their teacher than out of genuine interest.[9]

The other side of the problem is that CETs who perceive evangelism as one of their primary roles are often under at least some pressure—either internal or external (coming from supporting churches, the sending agency, other CETs, etc.)—to produce results by leading at least a few students to Christ. Just as students may feel pressure to respond favorably to the teacher's evangelistic efforts, a CET may feel pressure to count all expressions of interest in Christianity as genuine rather than questioning their sincerity. A CET may also be tempted to make the most of each expression of interest when sharing with other Christians about the fruits of his or her work. Far be it for me to suggest that God can never work through such scenarios such as those above to lead people to a genuine faith in Christ—I'm sure it can and does happen. But it would be irresponsible in such situations not to be wary of the potential for self-deception and even the abuse of power.

Power is an inherent part of the role of the teacher, so the solution to the problems created by the teacher's authority cannot lie in CETs somehow divesting themselves of this authority and influence. Neither does it lie in ignoring or denying the existence of this power. However, the solution also cannot be found in CETs' stifling their Christian witness for fear that it will be corrupted or tainted by the power of their role.

There are no easy answers to the problems posed by this situation, but I would suggest two concrete ways in which CETs can minimize problems. The first of these is a willingness to look honestly and even critically at the motivation of those students who seem to show interest in Christianity. Naturally CETs are eager to see such interest, but they should not let this cloud their ability to see clearly. When interacting with CETs, student interest in Christianity may be motivated by a variety of factors, and some of these have little to do with interest in God or Christianity per se. CETs will naturally feel the desire to interpret any expressed interest in Christianity as the workings of the Spirit and the fruit of their Christian witness. However, CETs also need to consider the possibility that what is really happening is that students have noticed how the teacher responds to their interest in the teacher's faith, and that they are in turn responding to the teacher's expressions of favor or enthusiasm rather than to the call and claims of the gospel. Granted, this may be a first step toward God, but CETs need to resist the temptation to portray such a step as more than it actually is.

Relationships with students who have already graduated from a CET's course are in many ways a more appropriate context for sharing about faith issues than relationships with students who are still in the CET's courses. Once students have left the CET's course, the relationship naturally becomes more equal—if nothing else, the CET is no longer in a position to grade the student—and this is a healthier context for any kind of personal relationship and sharing to develop in.

A second important way to deal with potential problems is through scrupulous attention to fairness and evenhandedness in dealings with students. As students become aware of a CET's desire to see interest in Christianity, they will no doubt also be very aware of whether or not the CET tends to give special attention and favor to those who express such interest. Just as power is a potential trap for the integrity of a CET's witness, it is also an opportunity to demonstrate that CETs are just and responsible in handling the power they have been given. If what students see in a CET is equal interest, care, and attention toward all students, no matter how they feel about the CET's faith, the witness of the CET will gain credibility from responsible handling of power and influence. It will also reflect the fact that God loves all of his children, not only those who have already responded to his call. Such evenhandedness may require a degree of self-discipline because some CETs' hearts may naturally incline more toward students who are interested in Christianity. But such impartiality is not only an essential part of avoiding the corrupting influence power can have on a CET's witness, it is also in and of itself an important element of that witness.

Being Identified as a Christian

As noted earlier, people in the host culture will often tend to see CETs first and foremost as Westerners rather than as Christians. Even when they do assume that CETs are Christians they may assume that Christian faith is simply an inherent part of Western culture rather than adherence to a faith which transcends all cultures. In most nations, CETs certainly cannot simply assume they will be viewed primarily as servants or emissaries of God or the church. If CETs are to be viewed as ambassadors of the church, they need to consider the question of how they can be publicly identified as Christians.

In their private lives, there are a variety of ways CETs can signal Christian allegiance. For example, public display of Christian symbols such as crosses or prayer before meals will to some extent serve to mark CETs as Christians, and may have value as a starting point for conversation. However, public display of symbols can also be relatively easily dismissed as a statement of cultural identity (or even just fashion) as much as one of faith. Perhaps more valuable is visible participation in Christian worship, whether this be with other Western Christians or with local Christians. Participation in local Christian churches is often more difficult than private worship with other Western Christians because of problems such as language barriers and differences in faith traditions. However, it has the advantage of publicly symbolizing the transcultural nature of the Christian faith, and is a natural way for CETs to identify themselves as Christians without reinforcing the idea that Christianity is a Western religion. (See chapter 8 for further discussion.)

Another vitally important way for CETs to identify themselves as Christians is by making their lives transparent and letting local people get close enough to see what makes them tick. This is closely tied in with what was said in chapter 3 about building relationships. If people have the chance to see CETs and get to know them, there should be opportunity for them to look into CETs' lives and see what is there. In settings where there is a legacy of suspicion toward Westerners, or where there is the suspicion that Western Christians have come to "sell" their faith, it is probably best for CETs to open their lives to local people and let local people take the initiative in examining CETs' lives at their leisure and on their own terms.

Of course, the effectiveness of such an approach depends entirely on the quality of the Christian life of the CET. If CETs allow their sense of goodwill toward the host culture to wane there may be little advantage to letting local people find out what the CETs really think. In contrast, Christians who truly live out their faith are an advertisement for Christianity which cannot be dismissed easily, even by a suspicious or hostile audience. As David Bosch notes, in Paul's time it was the "attractive lifestyle of the small Christian communities [which gave] credibility to the missionary outreach in which he and his fellow workers [were] involved."[10] Likewise, to the extent that the salt of Western Christians in the local community remains salty, their lives can build an important bridge between local people and the Christian faith, and even perhaps between the local Christian church and non-Christians in the community.

As to the question of publicly identifying themselves as

Christians in the classroom, I would argue that in general CETs can and should be open and forthright about their faith in class as the occasion arises. (Granted, public mention of Christianity is a far more sensitive issue in some host countries than others, so CETs should take their local situation into account as they interpret my comments about this issue. However, my sense is that there are few if any host countries where CETs are prohibited from being honest about the fact that they are Christians.) While CETs should not treat English classes primarily as a forum for preaching the Christian faith, neither should they be expected to leave their faith and beliefs at the door when they enter class, anymore than teachers of other persuasions would be expected to abandon their convictions during work hours.

In *Truth to Tell: The Gospel as Public Truth*, Lesslie Newbigin makes the compelling argument that the truth of the Christian gospel is not a personal truth which is to be confined to the private lives of Christian believers. Instead, it is truth that should be proclaimed and acknowledged in public life as well. As Newbigin argues, too often Christians have been trained to live in two different and separate worlds, a private one in which we can freely speak using Christian language and assumptions, and a public one in which Christian claims to truth need to be kept under wraps.[11] Yet, if Christian claims are true in any meaningful sense, their jurisdiction should encompass all of creation, not just the bits of territory enclosed by church walls. Thus, while CETs need not go to the extreme of what is often called Christian triumphalism, trumpeting the superiority of Christianity in ways that are more annoying than convincing, I would suggest that CETs can and should be honest and open about their Christian faith, even in the "public" domain of the English classroom.

In part this occurs through "owning" the Christian faith as the occasion arises, in response to a question or as CETs discuss issues with students. This may seem obvious, but for a number of reasons it doesn't always happen. First, there is the problem of external pressure. In some countries CETs are not permitted to advocate Christianity in the classroom, and in others there is widespread opposition or hostility to Christianity which would make its mention in class offensive. Second, some CETs may also feel internal pressure not to discuss their faith in class. As noted above, part of modern Western culture is the assumption that religious faith is a private, personal issue that should not be intruded into public settings such as the classroom (although the same rule seems not to apply equally to modern secular worldviews). Growing up in this culture, many Western Christians have internalized these rules about where it is and is not appropriate to allude to one's faith. The result is that many instinctively tend to avoid mention of Christian faith when in the classroom. In Western culture, prejudice among non-Christians and Christians alike against hard-sell or pushy approaches toward evangelism have also made many Christians reluctant to give anyone an excuse to accuse them of proselytizing. As a result they tend to be scrupulously low-profile about their faith in public settings.

However, if the Christian faith is truly an important shaping force in CETs' lives it is incumbent on them to honestly and openly acknowledge this faith in class when it is relevant to issues under discussion. This does not mean that CETs need feel compelled to shoehorn mention of Christianity into any and all class discussions. But when they share their views of issues or discuss their motivation for serving as CETs, it would be almost dishonest not to acknowledge the role Christianity plays in shaping what they believe and the decisions they make.

Owning Christian faith publicly does not mean that CETs need to come across to students as preachy. It may also be more comfortable for both CETs and students if CETs couch mention of their faith as "I messages," explicitly prefacing such statements by saying "This is what I believe" or "This is what many Christians believe" and thereby suggesting recognition of and respect for other views students may have. However, if CETs are to be transparent and honest about who they are and what they believe, they must be willing to own and acknowledge their Christian faith in the public setting of the classroom as well as in private discussion. If criticized for public mention of Christianity, this approach also gives CETs a good basis from which to explain and defend why they talk about their faith. When CETs need to justify mention of Christianity in class, appealing to the need to be honest has fewer negative side effects than resorting to the excuse that it is necessary to talk about Christianity because it is a part of Western culture. Such an approach also not only makes Christian witness public (the lamp on the stand), but in and of itself bears witness to what CETs believe about God's love of the truth.

5

English Teaching as Ministry

In the previous chapter I suggested that addressing students' need to learn English as diligently and professionally as possible is an essential aspect of CETs' witness. This chapter continues the theme of meeting students' needs as a way to demonstrate God's love and also bear witness to the essential characteristics of the Christian life, but with the focus now expanded to a broader range of needs.

In "Liberation Through Phonetics," Henry Bergen tells the story of "Ida," a young woman from the countryside who Henry and his wife, Bettie, taught in China. When Ida first became their student, she was withdrawn, sad, and silent. Whenever called on to speak in English, her responses were halting, uncertain, and accompanied by considerable embarrassment. She had special difficulty with pronunciation, and seemed to be headed toward failure in that subject, so the Bergens offered to give her extra coaching in phonetics and pronunciation.

As they came to know Ida better, they discovered that her lack of confidence was rooted in her childhood experiences as much as in any special difficulty with English. When she was young, her family was forced by financial difficulties to "sell" her to another family who wanted her as a future bride for one of their sons, an experience that left her feeling rejected and worthless. Eventually through hard work and persistence she was able to graduate from middle school and gain entrance to a teacher training college, hence escaping the arranged marriage. However, she could not so easily leave behind the poor self-image that the experience had caused her to form.

Ultimately the extra coaching sessions paid off, as Henry notes, as much because of the extra encouragement and moral support as because of the phonetics training. Ida was able to pass her phonetics examination, and over the next two years she went on to make substantial improvement in her spoken English before graduating. As Henry concludes: "Ida has been teaching now for a year. It has been a real pleasure to have had a small part in helping restore a beautiful soul's sense of worth and help her along, if only a little, in her search for truth and meaning."[1]

Obviously not all students taught by CETs have been through experiences as dramatic as Ida's, but to a greater or lesser extent they all come into the English classroom with needs that go beyond problems with English grammar. In this chapter I argue that one important way CETs can live out God's love is by being aware of their students' needs and viewing English teaching as an opportunity to minister to those needs. Discussion below will focus on how CETs can minister to a number of student needs that are especially relevant to language learning. However, much as the Bergens were able to bring an element of healing to Ida's life that affected more than her English study, CETs will find that ministry which starts with students' needs as learners may at times have beneficial impact on other areas of students' lives.

Secondarily, I will argue that the ways CETs teach embody messages about the Christian faith. CETs carry out their work in front of a student audience that is usually attentive and sometimes quite critical, and students will often base their opinions about what CETs really believe and value more on what they see CETs do than on what CETs say about their beliefs. It is therefore important for CETs to examine their teaching practices with an eye to the subtle messages these practices can send about what CETs believe.

Below we will consider several major areas of need which affect language learners, and discuss teaching approaches through which teachers can minister to these needs. Before plunging in, however, I feel the need to make several disclaimers. First, this discussion of ministering to students' needs is not intended to be exhaustive. While the particular needs addressed here are important, they are obviously not the only needs language learners have, so I hope the discussion below will encourage CETs to consider other ways in which they can minister to students' needs through their teaching.

Second, the discussion below is not intended to suggest divine sanction for contemporary assumptions about language teaching, particularly the communicative approach. While I will discuss how certain approaches to language teaching reflect aspects of Christian belief, I do not intend to suggest that these approaches are the only ones consistent with Christian faith. Clearly neither the Bible nor Christian tradition presents an explicit model of how any language should be taught, let alone modern English. Teaching practices other than those discussed below may very well also echo important aspects of Christian thought and teaching.

Finally, I do not contend that the teaching practices discussed below are exclusively Christian; in fact, to a large extent they are similarly compatible with humanism and a variety of other worldviews.[2] What I do contend is that CETs' approaches to language teaching can and do send students messages about what CETs believe, and that these messages should be compatible with what Christian teachers profess to believe. I also believe that by being aware of these messages, and emphasizing in practice those value messages which are consistent with Christian faith, CETs can present a good contextualized model of how the Christian faith should work itself out in daily life. Ultimately what should be most distinctive about the work of Christian teachers is not a particular set of teaching practices, but rather a sense that teaching is a calling to service and ministry, a Christian vocation rather than just a job, an opportunity for making

God's love a concrete reality to students rather than an abstract concept.

Communication and the Need for Respect

In this section, I will argue that by genuinely communicating with students in class, especially listening to them and taking their ideas seriously, CETs can demonstrate respect for students and enhance their sense of self-worth. Moreover, I would suggest that by doing this CETs accurately reflect the importance each individual person has in God's eyes.

Over the last two decades, the English teaching profession has placed increasing emphasis on the importance of genuine communication in the language classroom. More and more, as students practice English, teachers encourage them to use the language to express their own thoughts and ideas, and also to listen to the thoughts and ideas of others. As obvious as this emphasis on communication might seem, it has not always been widely accepted by language teaching theorists. In fact, it was not so long ago that language teaching in Western countries was based heavily on drills which required students to manipulate grammar structures with more attention to form than meaning. Also, for a number of reasons, genuine communication is still more conspicuous by its absence than its presence in many EFL classes around the world.[3] One reason is that in many countries local English teachers have a better command of the vocabulary and grammar rules of English than they have of the ability to use English communicatively, and this discourages them from encouraging communicative use of English in their classes. Another problem in many countries is that teachers are under pressure to prepare students for examinations which focus more on grammar and vocabulary than on practical communication skills, so teachers must spend most of their class time drilling students in order to prepare them for tests.

Bringing an emphasis on communication into the EFL classroom has a number of important advantages, one of the most important being that English study becomes more interesting and appealing. Even under the best of circumstances it isn't much fun to memorize, do drills, and try to make sense of English verb tenses. When the only chances to talk with other students consist of parroting awkward little dialogues there is little in English class to arouse enthusiasm. In contrast, students generally find English class more enjoyable if they have real opportunity to communicate with each other. Greater opportunity for communication in the EFL classroom also helps students see English as a vital communication tool rather than just an arcane code of little value except as a vehicle to good test scores.

There is, however, a third advantage that is related to the idea of students' need for respect and self-worth. When a teacher's main interest in listening to students is to determine whether what they say is grammatically correct, students quickly pick up the (presumably unintended) message that what they mean is not particularly important—the main thing is not to make a mistake with the third person singular verb ending. As such messages accumulate over time, it is all too easy for students to begin to feel that who they are, and what they feel and believe, is not particularly important either. In contrast, when the teacher listens to students' ideas, demonstrates interest, and encourages other students to pay attention as well, the implied message is that students' ideas—and students themselves—are of value. To the extent that they genuinely communicate with students, listening to them as well as speaking to them, CETs have the opportunity to build students' sense of self-worth.

Genuine communication with students is also a way for CETs to reflect the Christian conviction that each person is of value in God's eyes. In Scripture this idea of the value of each person is indicated by the remarkable fact that throughout history God has dealt with individual people as well as tribes and nations. For example, consider the statements in Scripture that God knows each person even in his or her mother's womb (Ps. 139:13-16), and knows the number of hairs on each person's head (Matt. 10:30-31). God also calls on people individually as well as corporately to come to him in prayer with even mundane matters such as their need for daily bread (Luke 11:3).

God's willingness to deal with people personally is also apparent in the way Jesus interacted with those he met. I sometimes marvel that, in an age when writing materials were expensive and difficult to come by, the authors of the Gospels devoted much of their precious stock of materials to recording long conversations between Jesus and various people he encountered. Perhaps the best examples are Jesus' conversations with Nicodemus and with the woman at the well in Samaria (John 3:1-21 and 4:1-42). In part, this no doubt reflects the fact that interaction and dialogue were an important part of Jesus' approach to teaching. It also reflects the fact that he gave time and attention to individuals, listening to them as well as preaching to them. This is a model CETs would do well to emulate.

In one sense, this issue of communication in English classes is generally not a major problem for CETs because they tend to be naturally more inclined to use English communicatively in class than most of their local colleagues will be. For one thing, just by virtue of the fact that they are native speakers of English, CETs will be more comfortable using English communicatively; in fact, many CETs have no choice other than to use English for much or all of their interaction with students. The presence of Western English teachers thus naturally enhances the "English atmosphere" of the school, and this is one of the main reasons why schools in many countries are so eager to have native speakers on their English department faculties—even those untrained as professional language teachers.

The fact that CETs are outsiders to the local culture also encourages real communicative activity in class because there is such a large natural "information gap" between CETs and their students. Students know a great deal of useful and interesting information about their country which is unfamiliar to CETs, and CETs have a corresponding range of knowledge about their own country which is unfamiliar to students. In other words, there is a great deal that CETs and their students have to talk about as they get to know each other. This information gap can be used to good advantage if English class becomes a place where CETs and students learn about each other's countries and cultures, using English as the medium of communication. (As noted in chapter 3, interest in learning about students' culture is also an important way of demonstrating respect for their culture.)

Even so, it is still important for CETs to be intentional about genuinely communicating with students in class, especially about taking the time to listen to them. The large class sizes which characterize many EFL settings often make it difficult for CETs to get to know students—even to learn their names—and may also foster a depersonalized atmosphere which discourages genuine communication. It is also very easy for both teachers and students to get so caught up in the forms of language, and to become so obsessed with mastering accuracy that the purpose of language—the sharing of information, ideas, and feelings—becomes lost. If this happens, something else very important is also lost—the opportunity for CETs to let students know they matter as people, and that what they think, feel, and believe is worthy of attention.

One of the joys of teaching English is that it presents a virtually unequaled opportunity for classroom communication with students. While some other subject matters lend themselves to lecture formats in which the teacher need have little interaction with the student audience, the very essence of language learning is mastery of a communication skill, and inherently calls for interaction between student and teacher that can cover an enormous range of interesting topics. When CETs really communicate with students, students develop a sense of worth that may impact them more than any particular point of language a CET might teach. As they take the time to listen to students, CETs also reflect their belief in a God who, despite his exalted position as lord of the universe, still attends to individual's prayers.

Empathy and the Need for Compassion

In this section my argument is that language learning is often a discouraging process for students, and that CETs should show compassion and develop the ability to empathize with students in their struggle. In this way, CETs not only minister to students, but also reflect God's compassion for humankind.

Language learning is an emotionally demanding process, and ultimate success depends to a large extent on the ability of learners to weather challenges to their resolve. One such challenge arises from the sense of vulnerability which accompanies efforts to learn a new language, especially learning to speak it. Much of a person's sense of self-esteem is based on the ability to handle social situations competently and to express oneself intelligently, skills which are very much based in command of language. The problem in learning a new language is that students have to give up their adult language competence and revert to a childlike stage of expression and comprehension skills. Put bluntly, students need to be willing to sound like fools as day after day they fumble through conversations—often in front of an audience of classmates—using a language over which they have at best shaky control. This can be quite embarrassing, and many learners ultimately choose to minimize the discomfort by speaking English as little as possible.

A second affective challenge language learners often face is discouragement. Mastery of English is a long arduous task which requires years of sustained effort, and it is very common for learners to become discouraged and simply give up. Discouragement is especially likely when learners feel they are making little progress. This problem occurs frequently during the intermediate stages of English study when the initial excitement of learning a new language has long since dissipated but when learners still haven't mastered enough English to do anything interesting or rewarding with it. It is also especially common in countries where there are few opportunities for students to use the English they learn. Lack of opportunity to use English denies students the encouragement that can come from successful attempts to use the language, and also gives English study an air of unreality.

These affective challenges faced by students need to be taken seriously by CETs. In fact, Douglas Brown suggests that one of the main tenants of a language teacher's creed should be the "warm fuzzy" principle: "All second language learners need to be treated with affective tender loving care."[4] To some degree, responding to students' vulnerability is a matter of common sense and consideration; for example, being gentle when correcting a student's grammar mistake, offering encouragement as well as corrections on compositions, and so forth. However, at a deeper level this "warm fuzzy" principle requires more than being nice to students. It also calls for empathy and compassion, an attempt on the part of CETs to put themselves in their students' shoes and understand what students experience and feel as they go about the task of learning English. This attempt is important not only for enhancement of CETs' own understanding and sensitivity, but also because it demonstrates a concern for students that goes beyond the quality of their academic performance.

It is by demonstrating compassion and empathy that CETs can most fully reflect key elements of the gospel. One of the greatest scandals and glories of the Christian faith is that God did not hold himself apart from humankind and issue commands from on high, but rather in the incarnation came down to the human level to share human life, joys, and trials. The original meaning of the word "compassion" is "to suffer with." Through his life and death this is exactly what God in Jesus Christ did for all humankind. At the foundation of Christian faith therefore lies an imperative for Christians to do for others what God did for humankind. Christians are not called to dispense goodwill from a distance, but rather to place themselves alongside others and share their joys and sufferings. Christians have no monopoly on empathy, but it is certainly true that Christians have a powerful role model of the importance of reaching out to others and sharing their lives. This imperative should inform Christians' work as language teachers as much as it does other aspects of their lives.

To a greater degree than CETs may realize, the simple act of choosing to go and teach in a foreign country is an important contribution toward students' ability to generate and sustain interest in English study. As noted earlier, just by virtue of being native speakers and "real" Westerners, the presence of CETs helps bring the study of English to life for students and makes it seem more real and exciting. In many host countries few students have previously had the opportunity to talk to English-speaking foreigners, so simply by being present CETs give students a vitally important chance to try out their English on a real Westerner and have the thrill of seeing it work. The presence of CETs helps boost not only students' levels of interest, but also their confidence, and this is a contribution to students in EFL settings that CETs should not underestimate.

A brief digression: In host countries where Western teachers and their teaching approaches are relatively rare, CETs can often generate a positive, enthusiastic response from students through a combination of active in-class methods and the sheer novelty of their presence. This can tempt CETs to rely on a teaching approach that consists of a mixed bag of fun activities and games drawn from an assortment of resource books. Such courses are initially quite popular with students, but over time students often come to feel a lack of direction and progress, a sense that they are busy but not quite sure where it is all leading. In order to sustain students' interest and enthusiasm, teachers need to have a well-structured plan including clear goals and evaluation strategies.

A related problem CETs must be careful to avoid is resentment from local teachers. When CETs' courses become popular among students, it is very easy for local teachers and their courses to look bad by comparison. Unfortunately it is not unheard of for Western teachers to exacerbate the problem by looking down on traditional teaching approaches used by local teachers and even making disparaging remarks about them. CETs need to recognize that traditional teaching approaches do have their virtues—one very practical advantage being that they are generally relatively effective in preparing students for the tests that so often determine their futures. The call to empathy and compassion also includes CETs' appreciating the difficulties local colleagues face, especially when teaching a language which is not their own.[5]

Let us return here to the main line of argument. Being native speakers makes it easier in some ways for CETs to help sustain students' enthusiasm for English study. However, as pointed out in chapter 3, native speakers may also have a relatively hard time understanding and empathizing with students' difficulties in the struggle to learn English. In comparison to local teachers, who usually have vivid memories of the obstacles they struggled to overcome as they learned English, native speakers of English will likely find it difficult to identify with the difficulties students face.[6] To be sure, empathy in the classroom is in part an issue of being attentive to students' feelings, recognizing them, and responding to them. In class this may mean something as simple as occasionally pausing to ask how everyone is doing or offer a word of encouragement. But empathy and compassion are also based in a genuine ability to place oneself in the students' shoes and to see, with some degree of accuracy, how the learning experience looks and feels from their perspective.

The ability of CETs to have compassion for students— "to suffer with" them—cannot be achieved through good intentions alone; it also requires a conscious effort on the part of CETs to learn as much as possible about what the experience of language learning is like for students. One way CETs can do this is by talking with students and learning about their lives. What CETs need to learn goes far beyond students' feelings about the most recent lesson in their English books. CETs also need to develop a sense of students' hopes and dreams, the price they paid to have an opportunity for education, their feelings about schools and teachers in general, and anything else in their lives that could impact their feelings about English study. Genuine compassion involves getting to know students as well as possible.

As argued in chapter 3, the other way CETs can develop more empathy and compassion for language students is by regularly engaging in language learning themselves. There is much insight into language learning and teaching that CETs can gain by being language learners themselves, but this requires a significant degree of compassion in the original sense of the word—getting down in the trenches and slogging it out just like the students do. As CETs try to learn the local language, they can experience making fools of themselves in public—and learning to laugh at their own mistakes while they learn from them. They can expect to be confused at times when they are overwhelmed with new information—and to have the joy of success when something puzzling suddenly becomes clear. They will no doubt experience discouragement and the temptation to give the whole endeavor up—but will also experience the deep satisfaction of growing mastery of a skill that opens new windows on the world.

The better CETs understand their students and the difficulties students face in language learning, the better CETs will know how to encourage their students or when to offer the right word of praise. Also, the very fact that a CET attempts to better understand students and their experience is often a source of encouragement to students. Finally, by making the effort to develop empathy and compassion for their students, CETs reflect the compassion God has for all people. It may well be that students will remember this model of compassion long after they have forgotten any particular point of English syntax a CET taught.

Motivation and the Need for Purpose

In this section I argue that one important way for CETs to minister to students is by helping them develop a stronger sense of purpose to motivate their language study. This not only helps sustain them along the long road to mastery of English, but also reflects the Christian conviction that life does indeed have purpose and meaning.

I will also briefly discuss the major types of motivation which professionals in the language teaching profession tend to draw on in efforts to motivate students. CETs need to be aware of the assumptions underlying these different approaches to motivating students because much discussion of motivation within the EFL field assumes a naturalistic worldview that seems to leave little room for God. I will argue that CETs should still draw on these ideas in order to help students develop a stronger sense of motivation, but that they should be careful not to implicitly endorse the naturalistic assumptions underlying these theories. Rather, by presenting students with alternative rationales for English study, CETs' goal is both to underline the importance of looking for purpose in language study—and, by implication, in anything else a student does—and to encourage students to search more widely for purpose.

Many students CETs encounter already have both motivation and a clear sense of purpose in their study of English, but there will be a great many others who have little or no idea why they are learning English, and consequently lack motivation. The essence of the problem for many students is that they only study English because they are required to—and they will cheerfully abandon it as soon as they are given the opportunity. These feelings about English study are particularly common in state school systems where study of English is required rather than optional. In such settings, students have never had to make a choice about whether to study English or not, so they have often not thought much about the desirability of doing so. This lack of rationale on students' part, combined with the fact that the value of knowing a little English in the midst of a non-English speaking environment is often less than obvious, causes many students to view English study as an enforced academic exercise of little practical value.[7]

One of the main tasks of an English teacher, especially in an EFL setting, is to build students' sense of motivation and drive by helping them find good reasons for studying English. Within the EFL profession, discussion of motivation tends to center on three basic kinds of rewards:[8]

Extrinsic rewards: One way for CETs to help students develop a sense of purpose in English study is to stress the practical benefits of learning English. These can range from very immediate benefits such as good test scores to longer-term rewards such as enhanced prospects for educational advancement or better jobs. The motivation inspired by such benefits is referred to as "extrinsic motivation" because the rewards come from outside the learner.

The usefulness of extrinsic rewards in motivating students of English is diminished somewhat by the tendency of their motivating force to dissipate quickly once the immediate goal is achieved. For example, once a test is over, students lose much of their drive to study—at least until the night before the next test. Another problem is that material rewards for success in English study are a long way off for most students, and the pull these rewards exert is weakened dramatically by their distance. For example, the possibility of a good job five years in the future may seem too remote to motivate a student to study today. However, such rewards have the significant advantage of being relatively concrete. It takes little imagination on students' part to see how, for example, enhanced job prospects might be a good thing. Also, some extrinsic rewards, such as test scores, are relatively immediate.

While students usually have some general idea of the ways in which learning English may enhance their lives, these benefits may seem rather hazy and distant in their minds. By giving students a clearer idea of the benefits that may await them, and reminding them of these benefits from time to time, CETs can help keep students' diligence in English study from flagging. To this end it is important for CETs to gain a realistic knowledge of what opportunities mastery of English opens for students in the host country. CETs can also help make these opportunities and benefits more real to students by bringing evidence of their existence into the classroom, for example, in the form of job advertisements or announcements of study opportunities. It can also be useful to invite local people who have benefited from learning English to come into class and talk about their experience as both learners and users of English. The more the external rewards of learning English seem real to students, the more likely these are to help students build and sustain a sense of purpose in their English study.

Intrinsic rewards: A second approach to building students' motivation—and one more often promoted in recent Western textbooks on language teaching—involves encouraging students to develop a sense of self-satisfaction in language study. Western theorists of human behavior such as Edward Deci and Abraham Maslow argue that "intrinsic motivation"—i.e., internal rewards such as feelings of achievement or self-satisfaction—is an especially powerful force driving human behavior.[9] Intrinsic motivation does not vanish once a particular goal is achieved, and the rewards it offers are also more immediate than most external rewards are, so intrinsic rewards do a better job of motivating *sustained* effort. Furthermore, and perhaps more surprisingly, intrinsic rewards also seem to be a more powerful driving force than external rewards. In other words, students who study out of a desire for personal achievement or satisfaction will generally work harder than those who study only because of a desire for good test scores or the hope of a future job.[10]

Helping students develop intrinsic motivation is sometimes easier said than done. In many school systems the world over, students have been trained for years (implicitly or explicitly) to view high test scores as the main goal of their English study, and are therefore accustomed to relying on external rewards as the force behind their study efforts. There are, however, a number of ways CETs can help students develop a greater sense of intrinsic motivation:

- By helping students see their progress more clearly. Helping students become more vividly aware of their progress in English study increases the chance that a sense of progress and achievement will motivate them in their study of English. To this end, grades are less useful than opportunity for "then and now" comparisons that allow students to see how much their English skills have progressed over a period of time. Ways to do this include keeping compositions students write at the beginning of a course for comparison with compositions at the end, taping interviews with students at the beginning of a semester to compare with interviews at the end, and so forth. (Granted, the effectiveness of this approach is based on the assumption that students actually will make progress over the course of a semester or a school year. In order to maximize the chance that visible improvement will take place, it is best to allow students a considerable period of time in which to make progress between the "then" and "now" measurements.) The more students have a sense of growing mastery of English, the more likely it is that the self-satisfaction this provides will become a major factor in motivating their English study.[11]

• By helping students "own" their English learning process. CETs can increase students' sense of satisfaction in English study by allowing them more voice and ownership in the process. If students are only going through the motions of a study effort dictated by someone else, they are not likely to have much personal investment or satisfaction in the results. In contrast, if students "own" their study of English, they are more likely to take a personal sense of pride and self-satisfaction in it. The more CETs allow students to make their own choices in English study with regard to goals, methods, and so forth, the more sense of ownership students will have in the process and the more they will feel that achievements are their own.

• By encouraging students to use English to pursue goals they are personally interested in. When students' study of English can be harnessed to their personal interests, they are more likely to find gratification in it. Ultimately the point of learning any new language is that it gives learners access to a whole new world of information, ideas, perspectives, ways of thinking, and relationships with people. When, for example, students discover they can use English to read books they want to read, watch films they like, talk with people they find interesting, and so forth, they are more likely to find the process interesting and rewarding enough that it is worth sustained effort.[12]

Approval from others: The tendency of Western theorists to assume that the most powerful drives are based on intrinsic rewards such as the desire for self-satisfaction, or, in Maslow's term, self-actualization, may carry a degree of Western cultural bias. Such rewards may be more powerful motivators for people in individualistic Western cultures than they are for people in cultures that are not so individualistic. For example, research conducted in Asian contexts suggests that for people in less individualistic cultures—i.e., the kinds of cultures in which most CETs work—desire for approval from one's social group is a more powerful motivating force than more self-oriented drives.[13] Even research conducted in Western cultures has concluded that positive feedback from another person, particularly feedback which enhances an individuals' sense of accomplishment, is a form of reward which has motivating power equal to that of the intrinsic rewards discussed above.[14]

Of course, feedback given by other people is not always positive, and negative feedback can be a significant factor in discouraging English study (or anything else). However, positive feedback is very effective in motivating study because it is both powerful and relatively immediate—teachers, family, classmates, and so forth are generally close at hand to provide prompt reinforcement.

The most obvious way CETs can make use of this type of reward to motivate students is through the positive feedback they offer to students, whether this be in the form of approving comments on students compositions, encouragement and praise in class, or affirming comments after a student interview. Such positive feedback tends to be more helpful and credible if it is specific enough that students can actually pinpoint what they did well (as opposed to generic nice comments that the teacher seems to hand out freely as a matter of course).

CETs can also create opportunities for students to get positive feedback from other people (classmates, other students, people in the community at large) by giving students the chance to display their skills and achievements through public display of what they have learned. Ways to do this include speech contests, plays, student newspapers, compilations of student compositions, and so forth. While these kinds of projects often require an additional investment of time and effort on the part of both students and teachers, they have the beneficial effect of allowing students' efforts to be affirmed in public forums, and the motivating effect of such opportunities makes this time and effort well invested.

With regard to these different types of rewards, and how CETs may employ them to help students develop a stronger sense of purpose and motivation, there are several points I wish to make:

- The first and most basic is that CETs should emphasize the question of purpose in their English classes, especially with students whose study of English—and perhaps study of other subjects—seems to lack any sense of drive and goal. Regular in-class discussion of different possible purposes for English study has the important effect of making students ever more aware of the issue of purpose in language study. The more often students are exposed to the question "Why?" the more likely they are to begin asking that question themselves and actively seeking an answer. Students' ultimate success in learning English will often be determined more by their sense of purpose and motivation than by any other single factor. The more students' attention is focused on the issue of purpose, the more likely they are to seek for and find a purpose that is sufficient to sustain their language study.

Emphasizing the importance of purpose in English study also indirectly suggests that purpose is something which exists and is worth seeking (a conviction which not all contemporary worldviews would endorse). By emphasizing this issue, CETs reflect the Christian belief that there is purpose to all aspects of life. Encouraging students to seek purpose in one area of life creates the possibility of a spillover effect in which they begin to reexamine the purpose of other aspects of their lives as well.

• In the effort to motivate students, I feel that CETs should draw on the motivational power of all three of the types of rewards described above. The practical benefit of using a mix of these rewards, as opposed to relying primarily on any single one of them, is that different students will respond to different kinds of rewards. One student may work hard mainly to please his parents, a second because she wants to score well on the final exam, and a third because she enjoys learning. By appealing to a variety of different rewards, rather than relying on any particular one, CETs increase the chance that each student in the class will find something he or she responds to.

There is, however, an additional reason why CETs should avoid relying on any single type of reward as the basis of a motivational strategy. As we pause to consider the three kinds of rewards mentioned above, we see that each assumes that purpose derives from within the natural, human world. Extrinsic rewards ultimately tend to be of the material variety, and if a CET relies too heavily on the promise of rewards such as good grades or (worldly) success in attempts to motivate students, it may seem to students that these are the main things the CET values. (Given the prevalence of materialism in Western culture, this is one point on which it is very important for CETs to make a distinction between Western culture and Christian belief.) With intrinsic rewards, it is the self which is the final source of reward and purpose, and overemphasizing intrinsic rewards may subtly suggest a worldview in which the individual human being is the ultimate standard and source of value. Approval from others is also a reward that derives from within the human, natural world, and overreliance on this approach to motivation may suggest a worldview in which there is no room for a standard or source of value beyond the human community.

In contrast, a Christian understanding would be that life has purpose and meaning going beyond material satisfaction, self-satisfaction, or the approval of other people. Growing up in the Reformed tradition (Presbyterian), I was expected to memorize the Westminster Shorter Catechism. Most of the Catechism never made it into my long-term memory, but I will always remember the first question and answer pair: Q: What is the chief end of man? A: To glorify God and enjoy him forever. In this simple statement are embedded two foundational Christian truths: (1) human existence has a purpose, and (2) this purpose derives from God rather than from within ourselves or from the world around us. This is not a view CETs will often have opportunity to articulate explicitly in class, although there may be occasions when stating this view directly is appropriate, particularly if it is directly relevant to class discussion. However, CETs want to avoid endorsing any particular approach motivation so enthusiastically that they seem to leave no room for a source of purpose and meaning that transcends the human world.

Each of the three kinds of rewards introduced above has genuine power to motivate, and each should be taken full advantage of. However, each of these kinds of rewards is at best only a partial reflection of life's ultimate purpose and rewards, and no single one should be endorsed as the "right" reason to study English. The advantage of presenting students with *all* these different potential rewards and reasons for studying English is that each one then becomes one alternative among many. Each can be used to stimulate students' search for purpose, but there is no suggestion that any single one in and of itself fully answers the question of purpose. This leaves room for—and may even hint at the existence of—other possible sources of purpose.

• CETs should encourage students to cast the net ever wider as they search for meaning in their study of English. The point of bringing specific kinds of possible rewards to students' attention is not to limit their consideration to these few possibilities. Rather, the point of suggesting specific possible rewards should be to broaden the range of possibilities for students by exposing them to ideas they may not previously have considered, and to encourage them to keep looking in ever wider and deeper ways for meaning. While CETs should encourage this for its positive impact on English study, it is also reasonable to assume that this search may have impact on other areas of students' lives, and may possibly move them toward asking more profound questions about the meaning and purpose of life itself. Obviously such a search does not always lead students toward God and the Christian faith, but if we truly believe that truth and meaning in life ultimately reside in God, we can only believe that the more students search for purpose in life, the more likely they are to find their way to God.

6

English Teaching as Christian Service

One of the main problems doctors in developing countries face in their struggle against disease is poor access to information. Especially when there is an outbreak of some new or unfamiliar kind of disease, it becomes vitally important that doctors can communicate with each other for information and advice, and also that they have access to medical data bases in other countries. In the book *The Coming Plague: Newly Emerging Diseases in a World Out of Balance*, Laurie Garrett tells how Nobel Peace Prize winning physician Dr. Bernard Lown set out to deal with this problem. With help from Russia, Japan, and Canada, he was able to set up a system called SatelLife that linked doctors in developing countries with each other by computer, and also linked them to data bases in medical libraries in Canada and the United States. By 1993, Zambia, Mozambique, and nine other developing countries were connected to the system, and SatelLife was playing an important role in the efforts of doctors in these countries to cooperate in combating disease.[1]

Garrett does not explicitly discuss the issue of language, but from her account it is quite clear that English plays a vital role in the effectiveness of the SatelLife system. For one thing, the data files to which the doctors are linked are written in English. For another, in order for doctors in these different countries to communicate with each other, they need a common language. From Garrett's description it appears that the language of choice in this international communication network—as in so many others—is English.

SatelLife is not a program begun by Christian missionaries, but its concern for the basic physical needs of the developing world is shared by Christian churches throughout the world, and there are countless Christian ministries that help the world's poor meet basic needs such as those for adequate food and water, health, employment, and education. Such ministries are an especially important aspect of the work of Western Christians in countries where there is a need for reconciliation between Western Christians and local people. In countries where people have negative feelings toward Western Christians, and perhaps toward Christianity in general, ministries of service not only meet physical needs but also suggest that Western Christians are concerned and willing to help even when they gain nothing by it. Ralph Covell argues that in cultures which are not well disposed toward the efforts of Christians, particularly Western Christians, the best witness is offered by a long-term stable church community engaged in "the full range of God's concern in ministries of education, medicine, and compassion."[2] John Stott suggests that the impact of such ministry is greatest when it comes with no strings attached, especially when it is not manipulated as an indirect means of evangelism.[3]

Stott also argues that the Christian model of mission should be found in the life of Jesus who, in addition to preaching, also engaged in ministries of service and compassion.[4] Jesus devoted much of his time and energy to activities such as healing the sick, and also taught his followers to engage in such ministries. We need only remember familiar passages such as the parable of the good Samaritan (Luke 10:25-37) in which Jesus makes a positive example of the good deeds of a Samaritan who helped a stranger in need, and which he ends by explicitly commanding his disciples to follow the example of the Samaritan. Likewise, in the parable of the sheep and the goats (Matt. 25:31-46) the righteous are praised for serving in very concrete and practical ways such as feeding the hungry, giving drink to the thirsty, offering hospitality to strangers, clothing the naked, and visiting prisoners.[5]

As is already evident in the passages cited above, while Jesus ministered to the needs of people from all stations of life, he consistently devoted special attention to the needs of those in society who were disadvantaged: the poor, the sick, and social outcasts like prostitutes, Samaritans, and tax collectors. These were the people with whom he spent much of his time and to whose needs he often attended. They were also the people he lifted up as models in parables such as the good Samaritan (Luke 10:25-37), Lazarus and the rich man (Luke 16:19-31), and the Pharisee and the tax collector (Luke 18:9-14), and in incidents such as the one in which the sinful woman washed his feet with her hair (Luke 7:36-50). This emphasis on the poor, powerless, and outcast is clearest in the Gospel of Luke, where Jesus announces his ministry by quoting Isaiah to the effect that he has come to preach good news to the poor, freedom to the captives, recovery to the blind, and release for the oppressed (Luke 4:18-19). This focus is also evident in the Lukan version of the Beatitudes (Luke 6:20-26) in which Jesus proclaims a blessing on the poor, the hungry, the sad, and those who are hated, a blessing which stands in stark contrast to the woe Jesus pronounces on those who are rich, well-fed, and without cares.[6] If, as John Stott suggests, we take the ministry of Christ as a model, Christians are called not only to minister to the needs of others, but also to pay special attention to the needs of those who are poor, outcast, and otherwise disadvantaged.

The question we will address in this chapter is: How can English teaching be a ministry of service that is even remotely analogous to healing the sick or feeding the hungry? I will argue that, as the opening anecdote suggests, English teaching is a service that makes a significant impact on people's ability to meet very concrete needs, and in this sense can and should be considered a ministry of compassion. However, the degree to which such a ministry has a distinctively

Christian flavor is dependent less on *how* CETs teach (unlike the previous two chapters) than on *who* CETs teach. My argument will be that it is important for CETs and sending agencies to give serious attention to the ways in which they can use their English teaching as a ministry to the poor and disadvantaged. I will not argue that this is the only basis on which sending agencies and CETs should decide where and who to teach, but I will suggest that this should be one of the important factors considered. If Western Christians wish the overall impact of their mission service to reflect the model presented by Jesus' ministry, service to the poor needs to be a prominent part of the overall effort.

English as a Key to Opportunity

Many Westerners, particularly from the United States, may not fully realize what a powerful impact learning English—or failing to learn it—can have on the lives of people throughout the world. In the United States, United Kingdom, and other English-speaking nations, views of language learning are often colored by memories of studying Spanish, French, or German in high school or college, where foreign language class was just one class among many and generally not a terribly important one. In English-speaking countries, failure to do well in foreign language classes does not generally make a dramatic impact on one's life, and this experience quite naturally tempts Western English teachers to view foreign language learning in other countries as equally optional.

What this view fails to recognize is that English is not just another foreign language. It plays a much larger role beyond its countries of origin than any previous language ever has. This is not only true in countries which were once colonies of English-speaking nations, where one might expect English to be more widely used, but also in many countries which were never colonies of an English-speaking nation and even in countries where the indigenous language is a major world language in its own right. Consider the following randomly selected examples of the role English plays in countries where very few people speak English as their first or native language:

Nigeria: Nigeria gained independence from British colonial rule in 1960, but even today English is still the most important subject on standardized examinations which students face at the end of secondary schooling. Command of English is required for admittance to university and also for many kinds of jobs.[7]

Philippines: The Philippines have been independent of United States colonial rule since shortly after the Second World War, but English is still used in most formal settings: government employment, college admission tests, and modern computer related businesses. Knowledge of English is necessary for most high-paying jobs, especially in business, and it is even important for securing relatively low-paying jobs such as those of many Filipinos who work overseas as domestic laborers.[8]

Hong Kong: During the years that Hong Kong was a British colony, virtually all secondary and tertiary education was English-medium. Since the reversion of Hong Kong to Chinese sovereignty in 1997, the Hong Kong government has promoted policies which would offer a much greater proportion of secondary education in Chinese. However, despite the fact that virtually all of Hong Kong's population speaks Chinese (Cantonese), these efforts have met considerable resistance. Parents still generally prefer their children to have an English-medium secondary education, in part because English is necessary for students who hope to study in one of Hong Kong's universities, and also because knowledge of English remains a necessity for many kinds of professional and business jobs.

Namibia: Unlike the above, Namibia was never ruled by an English-speaking colonial power, and the language imposed by its former colonial ruler—South Africa—was Afrikaans. However, black people in Namibia came to see English as the "language of liberation." At independence, a policy for the promotion of English in education and government was adopted. This policy has given considerable advantages in education and employment to those few Namibians who had previously had opportunity to learn English.[9]

Cameroon: Before independence in 1960, most of Cameroon was a French colony. Despite this fact, French has had to share the role of official language with English since independence, and it has become official policy to teach English in French-medium schools. There is considerable incentive to learn English because there are more job opportunities for people who speak English as well as French.[10]

China: Mandarin Chinese (*Putonghua*) is spoken as a native language by more people than any other language in the world, but in China English is still a required subject for all Chinese middle school and university students. English plays a decisive role in determining who has access to educational opportunities because it is one of the most important subjects on the standardized tests which determine who will advance up the educational ladder. Knowledge of English is also a great asset in seeking employment, particularly for high-paying jobs with joint-venture firms.

Tunisia: The official language of Tunisia is Arabic, one of the world's most widely spoken and important languages. Another international language—French—is also widely known. However, even here English plays a substantial role because it is necessary for advanced studies in science and technology.[11]

In different ways the examples above all reflect the reality that the world role of English has grown beyond its origins as an artifact of colonial rule. English has come to play an enormous role in international communication, and hence in providing (or denying) access to interaction with the world community and its resources. This role is further illustrated by the following facts:

- A great majority of the world's scientific and technological output is written in English. In any country, most academic journals with an international readership are published in English.
- A great majority of the world's international organiza-

tions function in English; no other language even comes close to English's level of dominance.

• English is the dominant language of the tourism industry, and all over the world shop signs, menus, safety instructions, travel information, maps, and road signs are to be found in English.

• English is the language of the sea and airline industries, and internationally used communication codes like "Seaspeak," "Emergency Speak," and "Airspeak" are essentially regularized and simplified forms of English.

• English dominates popular culture worldwide, especially popular songs and films.

• The great bulk of the world's electronically stored information is in English; a frequently cited estimate is 80 percent. English is also the preeminent language of the Internet.[12]

Because of the facts above, individuals who know English generally have much better access to education and employment opportunities than individuals who do not. Likewise, nations, regions, or social groups which have substantial English-speaking talent are in a much better position to take advantage of opportunities in technology, trade, tourism, communications, computers, publishing, shipping, diplomacy, media, and education than are nations or groups which are lacking in such talent. As Robert Phillipson concludes: "English, to a much greater extent than any other language, is the language in which the fate of most of the world's millions is decided."[13]

The implication of all of this for CETs is that teaching English is not just teaching a "foreign language" in a sense that would be familiar to most people from English-speaking nations. The fate of students in the host country's educational system, and their eventual ability to get and keep good jobs, may depend on how well they learn English. Likewise, the ability of a region, social group, or nation to interact and compete nationally and internationally may be dependent to a large degree on whether or not it has enough people with the English skills necessary to access the world's storehouse of information and to interact with the world community. As distant as such a reality may seem on a routine day in class, students' success or failure in English may have a very direct impact on how well they and even their people can put food on the table and clothing on their backs. The gift that CETs offer by teaching English can thus, in a very real sense, be a ministry of service which has powerful potential to help students and their communities to meet basic physical needs.

The Linguistic Imperialism Issue

The important role that English often plays in determining who does and does not have access to information, resources, and opportunity is underscored by an issue which has recently received considerable attention in the international English-teaching community: the issue of "linguistic imperialism." Up to this point our assumption has been that the service CETs offer by teaching English is generally beneficial to the people of the host country. However, here we will pause briefly to consider the arguments of scholars who view English and its promotion in a less favorable light. These scholars argue that the promotion of English is, in and of itself, a form of "linguistic imperialism" which benefits English-speaking nations and elites.[14]

In summary form, the critique of these scholars goes as follows: English attained its status as a world language as a result of almost two centuries of world dominance by English-speaking powers, first the United Kingdom and then the United States. Now, the dominant role which English plays in commerce, science, technology, and many other fields gives English-speaking nations and people a host of advantages. For example, because most of the world's technological information is published in English, English-speakers have more ready access to that information and the advantages it confers in technological competition. The fact that most international meetings are held in English also ensures that English-speakers will have a more dominant voice and role than those whose command of English is weaker. Even the English-teaching profession itself serves to illustrate the advantages conferred on English-speaking nations by the world role of English. Thousands of English teachers, not to mention book publishers and school administrators, owe their jobs to the dominance of English. No other language gives so many of its speakers employment in teaching and promoting their own language. Thus, in a range of ways, the promotion of English tends to help sustain a monopoly of power in the hands of English-speaking nations.

These scholars also argue that the dominant role of English tends to consolidate the power of elite groups in non-English speaking nations. It is often assumed that promoting English in non-English speaking countries will benefit these nations by helping them modernize. But critics point out that access to English in these societies is generally unequal, and that only the wealthy and powerful can ensure themselves adequate opportunities to learn English.[15] Within these societies, therefore, English is often less a route to advancement for the disadvantaged than it is a gatekeeper which denies them access to educational advancement and high-paying jobs. The upshot of all this is that the more dominant English becomes, the more power is concentrated in the hands of English speakers, and the implication is that the work of English teachers, including CETs, may in fact facilitate the perpetuation of oppressive and unequal distributions of power.

There are some aspects of this linguistic imperialism critique that I find problematic. For one thing, it seems to assign too important a role to the efforts of English teachers as a force in the continuing global spread of English. As I think even the critics themselves would agree, the primary driving force behind English's continuing spread is the tremendous technological, economic, military, and cultural power of English-speaking nations, and the growth of the English-teaching profession is more a consequence of that power than the source of it. I also have reservations about the critique's portrayal of English teachers as accessories to an act of imperialism, because this seems to suggest (by implication at least) that perhaps they shouldn't teach English at all. The problem with this suggestion, as at least one of the critics himself points out, is that if mastery of English provides access to opportunity and resources, the idea that English teachers should decrease access to it even further by giving up their jobs is unlikely to help the situation.[16]

My objections aside, however, I think there are two reasons why it is useful for CETs to give careful consideration to the issues raised in this linguistic imperialism critique. First, it underscores the point made in the previous section: Command of English gives a significant advantage to those who have such command, so CETs and sending agencies need to take seriously the potential for English teaching to be a potent form of social service and ministry.

Second, the overall impact of CETs' work has the potential to either strengthen the position of an elite, or to lessen the gap between the "haves" and "have-nots" by increasing the opportunities open to the disadvantaged. It is not within the power of CETs and sending agencies—or even the English-teaching profession as a whole—to turn back the worldwide spread of English, nor to prevent this spread from giving English speakers a competitive advantage in many fields of endeavor. However, CETs and sending agencies do have it within their power to minimize such impact by seeing that opportunity to learn English is as equally distributed as possible. This can only be done by making a conscious attempt to direct at least a portion of their ministry to the poor and disadvantaged. As we shall see below, this is not always easy to do, nor is it a task to which all CETs should necessarily feel called. However, if the English teaching mission effort of Western nations in any given host country seems to be disproportionately concerned with serving those in that society who are already relatively advantaged, something of the essential nature and message of Christian mission is lost. This is a danger worthy of serious consideration.

English Teaching as Ministry to the Poor
Defining "ministry to the poor"

CETs do not typically work with the poorest of the poor; in fact, many of the truly poor and oppressed of the world are not in a situation where studying English is a reasonable or efficacious prescription for the problems they face. A question we therefore need to consider is: In the context of English teaching, what is a reasonable definition of "ministry to the poor and disadvantaged"? I would suggest that the question sending agencies and individual CETs should ask in assessing their work as ministry to the poor is: By teaching in a given setting, do CETs extend opportunity to disadvantaged groups who might otherwise have been denied such opportunity? In other words, in light of the linguistic imperialism critique summarized above, does the work of CETs help equalize access to the wealth and power which knowledge of English can confer?

Needless to say, there is much CETs can do to help individual students who are poor and disadvantaged, but in determining where CETs should be placed, the question is less one of serving individual students than of serving broader populations. For CETs, "ministry to the poor" usually falls into one of the two following categories:

Category 1: Service to poor or disadvantaged nations: Some of the world's poorer nations are held back in their efforts to develop and modernize at least partially by a lack of people who have skills in English. In such nations "ministry to the poor" through English teaching might consist of providing English training for people in strategic areas of the economy so as to enhance the ability of the country to develop economically. Within such countries, for example, CETs might make a contribution by: teaching students in scientific and technical fields so that they would have better access to scientific knowledge in English; training translators so that businesses in the host country would better be able to participate in international trade; teaching tour guides and even hotel and restaurant staff so that the national tourist industry would more effectively compete on the international tourism market; even training community or development workers so that they would be better able to exchange information and experiences with similar workers in other developing countries.

For sending agencies or individual CETs engaged in this kind of ministry, it is important to remember that the goal is to benefit the host nation as a whole rather than just select individuals within that nation. Life in these nations is often difficult, and many students will want to learn English at least in part because of the hope it offers of escaping from the host nation and starting a new life in some other country, probably a developed English-speaking one. It is only natural for CETs in such settings to be sympathetic with the plight of individuals who want to leave, and it is not unusual for CETs to actively help some of their favorite students in their efforts to leave. However, CETs and sending agencies need to realize that such efforts tend to undermine the goal of training talent which will assist the host country in its efforts to develop, and they may also encourage local people to curry favor with CETs as a strategy for securing opportunities to go abroad.

One other problem in this kind of ministry is that it often involves CETs teaching students who are from backgrounds which, in the context of their nation, are relatively elite. As pointed out above, this creates the danger that the overall impact of CETs' ministry will be to help an elite class maintain its privileged status. In poor nations where a small elite is more concerned with maintaining its own power and privileges than with helping the nation as a whole, English-teaching service which trains members of the elite group may have little beneficial impact on the nation as a whole. However, in poor nations where the leading classes seem engaged in a genuine effort to develop their nation, a ministry of English teaching may result in benefit to a larger segment of the society, even if many of a CET's students still come from relatively privileged backgrounds.

Category 2: Service to poor or disadvantaged groups

within a nation: In many host countries, there are identifiable groups within the population whose access to educational and employment opportunities are limited by the dominant group because of their region, race or ethnic background, gender, religion, or other characteristics. In situations where these disadvantaged groups are cut off from opportunities in part because of inadequate training in English, CETs can have a valuable ministry by increasing such opportunities. Examples of this kind of service might include: teaching in a school for women or members of a disadvantaged ethnic minority, working in schools for the physically handicapped, or working in colleges which train teachers for service in poorer regions of the host country. To the extent that improved English training allows individuals from these groups to get better education and jobs and reach higher positions in the host society, these groups will have greater economic power and better access to social and political influence. This, in turn, may help break down barriers of prejudice against the group—or at least place the group in a better position to struggle against such barriers.

Ministries of this type may well touch on complicated social issues within the host society so it behooves CETs working in such ministries to learn as much as possible about the social context in which they work in order to assure that the training they provide will actually result in the benefits they are working toward. In particular, any assumptions about how much learning English will increase access to educational and employment opportunities need to take into consideration the other factors that work to limit such opportunities. For example, it would do little good to train women as business translators in a country where it is considered unacceptable for women to mix with men in the workplace. In such a setting English training geared toward another goal might be more efficacious.

CETs engaged in such ministries also need to be willing to accept the fact that enabling a few individuals from a disadvantaged group to gain better education or jobs will not always translate into direct benefits for the group as a whole.

As noted above, improved English skills sometimes serve as a ticket that enables individuals to escape the difficulties of their social setting rather than as a tool with which they better the situation of their group. However, even when English training permits individuals to escape, it is often the case that they continue to help their families and social groups in a variety of ways, especially if there is a high degree of solidarity and mutual assistance within the group. For example, students from poor regions whose English skills help them get good jobs outside the region may become an important source of income for family members back home, as well as a vital source of information and connections for others in their home area who seek educational or economic opportunity.

Needless to say, the two different categories of "ministry to the poor" presented above are not mutually exclusive, and may well be closely related to each other. An interesting example of this is provided by the Teachers Project of the Amity Foundation.[17] When the Teachers Project began in the 1980s, China as a whole was a relatively poor nation struggling to modernize and develop economically, so Amity responded to this need by placing most of its English teachers in large technological universities in major cities. By the 1990s, however, most of China's larger cities had experienced significant economic development, and the problem was less one of general poverty than of an increasing gap in prosperity between urban and rural areas. As a result, in the early 1990s Amity decided to redirect the focus of the Teachers Project and place English teachers mainly in small colleges that train teachers for rural junior secondary schools. One reason for this choice was that these colleges tend to be relatively poor, and lack channels for locating and hiring foreign English teachers. Another reason is that the poor oral English of teachers in many rural junior middle schools disadvantages students in these schools in competition for scarce places in senior middle schools, reducing these students' opportunities for further education.

Deciding where to place CETs

Determining what placements will enable CETs to make a genuinely effective contribution to the disadvantaged is not always a simple matter, and there are many things that individual CETs and sending agencies need to know in assessing a possible placement. Among these are the following:

- What need does the host country or region have for English speakers? Does the host country or region have need of English speakers in order to pursue goals of modernization or development?

- What are the backgrounds of students in the CET's host school? Are these students relatively poor in relationship to their society? Are they members of groups which are disadvantaged in some way?

- What role is played by English in the educational system? Is English a required subject for moving up the educational ladder? Do students need to pass English tests in order to graduate or enter the next level of education? Are there levels of education at which English becomes the medium of instruction?

- What opportunities are created by command of English? What opportunities will mastery of English create for students as individuals? How will students' families and communities benefit from students' improved opportunities to learn English?[18]

It is not always easy for individual CETs or even sending agencies to have the answers to questions such as those above before making decisions as to where CETs should be placed. CETs who locate their own placements often do so in countries with which they are not very familiar, and they may have less than comprehensive information about both the institution and society in which they will work. While sending agencies are often in a better position to gather information about possible placements over a period of time, their administrative offices may be located hundreds or thousands of miles away from the places to which CETs are sent, and their firsthand knowledge of any given placement may be confined to brief infrequent visits.

For the reasons above, sending agencies are often heavily dependent on their teachers to serve as their eyes and ears in the host country, helping the main offices maintain an up-to-date picture of needs in the host country and making sure that the agency has the information necessary to make informed decisions about the placement of future CETs. This, in turn, is another reason why CETs should make the effort to understand their host country as well as possible. The better CETs understand the host society, the more accurately they will be able to assess the overall impact of their teaching work in a given placement.

Are CETs Always Called to Ministry to the Poor?

So far in this chapter I have stressed the idea that English teaching can and should be viewed as a ministry to the poor and disadvantaged, perhaps even to the point of creating the impression that I believe the only legitimate Christian choice for *all* CETs is to work in positions where their work primarily benefits the disadvantaged. If so, this is where I will restore some balance to my argument by recognizing that there are also good reasons to teach students who are from more advantaged, even elite backgrounds.

One such reason, the idea that training an elite may benefit a poor nation as a whole, has already been mentioned above. A second reason why CETs may be placed in more prestigious institutions, where they will often teach students from relatively privileged backgrounds, is that such placements direct the witness of CETs to the more influential classes of the host culture. In countries where there is little indigenous Christian presence, or where the local Christian community is isolated from the mainstream and centers of power, this enables a Christian witness to be present at levels of society where there might otherwise be little Christian witness at all. If the witness of CETs in these positions is a positive one, it may also have the desirable effect of creating greater openness toward the Christian faith in the centers of power, even among people who might not personally have any interest in Christianity.

A third point is that a witness of professional excellence, such as suggested in chapter 4, may shine more brightly in places and locations where standards are higher and more challenging, and these would tend to be the best schools in a nation rather than those serving the marginal members of its population. The ability of Christians to perform well in such settings suggests that there is no necessary contradiction between Christian faith and modern professionalism.

We should also recognize that service in a relatively middle class or elite school does not preclude service to the poor. CETs often have the option of volunteering a portion of their free time to various forms of volunteer English-teaching service for less well-off populations. When there are no opportunities to serve the disadvantaged through English teaching, it is also sometimes possible for CETs to be involved in other forms of volunteer service to the poor (helping in orphanages, for example), or at the very least to financially support such efforts through contribution to local or international agencies involved in such work.

As noted in the introduction to this chapter, the model presented by Jesus' ministry suggests the need for CETs to serve people from all levels of the host society rather than exclusively with those from its lower levels. In fact, the overall witness of CETs in a host country probably shines at its brightest, and comes closest to replicating Jesus' own ministry, when it demonstrates both a level of quality which enables CETs to teach in the best schools, and also a level of compassion for the disadvantaged which compels them to seek out and serve the poor and marginal members of society.

However, on the whole there is relatively little danger that the needs of the host country's elites and its better schools will be underserved. Higher quality schools generally have better networks for recruiting CETs overseas, so are less likely to be overlooked when CETs search for placements. The better teaching and living conditions they usually offer also help ensure that they are given serious consideration, as does the higher prestige which teaching in such schools provides. Finally, market forces tend to channel both independent CETs and CET-sending agencies toward the service of those who can best afford to pay rather than those who are most in need. CETs who support themselves financially through their work (as opposed to those whose primary financial support comes from their home country) are naturally attracted to placements which can provide an adequate living. In many cases by working overseas CETs will already be accepting lower salaries than they would earn at home. In fact, some CETs working abroad barely break even over the course of a year, or even lose money. Naturally under such circumstances there are good reasons for CETs to seek teaching positions that pay adequately, not least because this makes it possible for CETs to remain overseas longer. Likewise, sending agencies are often short of funds, so they have an interest in placing CETs in institutions which can afford to cover much of teachers' costs, making it possible to support a larger number of CETs overseas with a relatively limited financial commitment from the sending agency. All of these factors combine to ensure that elite institutions generally have first choice of available CET candidates.

The greater danger is that the factors above would cause CETs and CET sending agencies not to devote enough attention and resources to the needs of poorer schools and disadvantaged members of the host society, and that the resulting ministry and witness would seem too worldly. As Paul Hiebert writes: "One key measure of the godliness of a society or a church is the way they treat the oppressed and marginalized. For its own advantage the world takes care of the successful, the powerful, and the wealthy. The church, however, is entrusted with the care of the poor, the widows, the orphans, the sick, the oppressed, the wayward, the spiritually immature, and the lost."[19] With only minor adjustments, the same statement could be made of the ministry of CETs and CET-sending agencies. As the linguistic imperialism debate should serve to remind us, a message is sent by the choices CETs and their agencies make as to whom to serve. If the ministry of CETs is disproportionately devoted to the wealthy and powerful in a society, helping them sustain their privileged position, then CETs may have a positive Christian witness to the particular students they teach, but the Christian message sent to society at large will be more muted and ambiguous. If, in contrast, CETs' efforts are also directed to those who are less able to reward and who need help more, the CET ministry will more clearly bear witness to the love of a God who gave without any hope of return.

Concern for the poor and disadvantaged is by no means confined to Christians. There are a variety of non-Christian volunteer agencies (such as the United States Peace Corps and the United Kingdom Voluntary Service Organization) which place English teachers in settings where they will serve the poor. We cannot and should not therefore claim that service of this nature is distinctively Christian. However, we can and should try to ensure that one of the distinctive characteristics of the service of CETs is concern for the needs of the disadvantaged. Given the factors which encourage Western teachers to take relatively high-paying and comfortable positions abroad—where they often serve a population which is also relatively comfortable—it is unusual and even noteworthy when Western teachers are sent to disadvantaged sectors of a society which cannot afford to pay well and do not necessarily have the best conditions or students. It is to the credit of Christians everywhere when people find that English teachers engaged in service that is more sacrificial than self-serving are Christians. Christians have a fine tradition of service to the poor and disadvantaged, and it seems only right that this tradition should inform decisions made by church groups and individual Christians as to where and how CETs should serve.

7

English Teaching toward Peacemaking and Intercultural Understanding

CETs as Peacemakers

The biblical concept of peace is more than an absence of quarrels. It is a state of reconciliation in which the issues which would divide nation from nation, person from person, and person from God have been laid to rest. It is a state in which people are "without spot or blemish" with regard to God, and presumably also with regard to each other (cf. 2 Pet. 3:14). This view of peace is stated most clearly and explicitly in Ephesians 2:11-19 where it is written that Christ makes peace between God and humankind through his sacrifice on the cross by destroying the hostility—the "dividing wall"—that separates God and humankind.[1] It is not enough that overt manifestations of conflict cease; the issues which give rise to conflict and divide people from each other must also be dealt with. As Miroslav Volf argues: "Much more than just the absence of hostility sustained by the absence of contact, *peace is communion between former enemies.*"[2]

Peace is sometimes described in Scripture as a blessing which God's people receive as a consequence of righteousness and obedience, but it is also something which they are called on to "seek" and "pursue" actively (Ps. 34:14). For God's people, one aspect of this task is doing all that is within their power to maintain peace among themselves (Mark 9:50; Col. 3:15; 1 Thess. 5:13) and also peace between themselves and other people (Rom. 12:17-19), not least because this is an important part of their witness (Heb. 12:14). However, Christians are expected to do more than maintain peace between themselves and others. In the same way that Christ through his sacrifice broke down the barriers between humankind and God, Christians are entrusted with the task of reconciling the world to God (2 Cor. 5:17-20), and one aspect of this is actively working toward the cause of peace in the world. As Jesus taught in the Sermon on the Mount (Matt. 5:9): "Blessed are the peacemakers, for they will be called children of God."[3]

The task of promoting peace between nations may seem rather remote from the daily classroom duties of a CET, but I would argue that promoting peace between people of different cultures should be one of the key missions of CETs, not least because of the kinds of countries in which most CETs serve. As noted in chapter 2, these nations are very different from the West culturally. Their peoples often do not have a good understanding of the West and its culture, and their cultures are in turn poorly understood by the West. Furthermore, these tend to be nations whose relations with the West are strained or even openly adversary. This point is underscored in a recent book by Samuel Huntington which argues that the main lines of division in the post-Cold War world are lines of culture rather than political ideology, and that large-scale conflict is more likely to occur between nations which differ from each other culturally than those which are similar. Huntington views the world as falling into a number of major cultural groupings ("civilizations"), and suggests that the civilizations with which the West is most likely to come into conflict are those of the Islamic world and China, and, to a lesser degree, Japan, India, and the Orthodox world (mainly Russia).[4] Significantly for CETs, Huntington's list of potential adversaries of the West corresponds rather closely (with the exception of India) to the list of places in which CETs are most likely to live and teach.

One way in which CETs are called to carry out a ministry of reconciliation in such nations is by serving as goodwill ambassadors, demonstrating through their presence and service that many in the West have concern for the well-being of people in the host country. In many host nations where CETs work, Westerners are relatively rare, and it is not unusual for a CET to be the first and perhaps only Westerner that students ever have an opportunity to interact with on a close and extended basis. In these situations, the presence of even a single CET can make a substantial impact on the attitudes students have toward the West.

We should be clear that the goal of this ministry of reconciliation is not to try to persuade people in the host country that the nations of the West are always virtuous in their actions or benign in their intentions; this assumption simply isn't true. The goal is rather to present a witness of love that transcends national identity. Through their willingness to work for understanding and peace between both their home and host countries, CETs can demonstrate a love that is not partial to one nation or the other, but rather encompasses both. Such a witness can be a powerful reflection of the impartiality of God's love. Another goal of this ministry of peacemaking is to provide evidence that, as would be the case with any nation, the self-serving impulses which drive the people and nations of the West are also leavened by desires and values that are more generous and less self-centered. This helps ensure that when incidents occur which strain relations between the host country and the West, people in the host country will resist the temptation to completely demonize the West (or a given Western nation), giving up on all attempts to reach mutual understanding and peaceful accommodation. (Needless to say, CETs' roles in this effort should go two ways—also helping people in their home countries gain a better and fairer understanding of the host country.)

The importance of such a ministry was driven home to me recently (1999) in a rather forceful way during visits to Western English teachers in China after NATO's bombing of the Chinese embassy in Yugoslavia. Chinese anger at the United States and other NATO countries was widespread and deep, especially among students. Coming on the heels of a series of other disputes between the United States and China, it fueled tendencies to see the United States as an "evil empire" bent on keeping China down. In such a situation, the presence of Western English teachers in China, a great many of them CETs, was a helpful reminder to Chinese people in general and students in particular of the goodwill many in the West bear toward China. These teachers probably helped prevent many students from concluding that the West's attitude toward China was one of unalloyed hostility. In part this was because discussions with Western teachers exposed many in China to perspectives on the incident that they might not otherwise have considered. However, the greater contribution CETs and other Western teachers made in this situation was one of simply being there—their presence serving as concrete evidence of a desire among many in the West to work toward better understanding and ties.

However, the calling of CETs to a peacemaker role goes beyond their function as goodwill ambassadors for the West. An inherent part of the work of CETs—and all English teachers—should be the promotion of better skills for intercultural understanding so that students in the host culture are better able to relate to people of any and all cultures, Western or otherwise. We need to recognize that the ultimate goal of English study is not simply mastery of the English language itself. To the extent that students learn English for genuine communication purposes, as opposed to just studying in order to complete requirements and pass tests, they learn English because they need it in order to interact either directly (face to face) or indirectly (through the medium of print, film, etc.) with people from other cultural backgrounds. Therefore, students need to learn more than just English grammar and vocabulary. They also need to learn intercultural communication skills which will enable them to effectively understand and communicate with people of other cultural backgrounds.

This being the case, one duty of English teachers is the important but demanding task of helping students develop skills for understanding people (books, articles, films, etc.) of other cultural backgrounds, and helping them become more proficient in interacting across cultural lines in ways which will maximize the possibilities of mutual understanding and harmony between people of different cultures, especially between groups whose past relationships have often lacked such qualities. Just as CETs' function as goodwill ambassadors demonstrates their concern for promoting better relations between their host and home countries, CETs' efforts to promote better skills in intercultural communication and understanding provide evidence of CETs' concern for the promotion of peace between people of all cultural backgrounds. Efforts to teach such skills can and should be seen as an indirect reflection of God's love for all people and his desire that they learn to coexist in peace.

Unfortunately, intercultural understanding and sensitivity are skills in which CETs have no inherent advantage by virtue of being natives of English-speaking countries. There is nothing in the history of the West's relations with the rest of the world to suggest that Westerners are any more naturally inclined to intercultural sensitivity and understanding than are people from any other culture. Even CETs who have had professional training in language teaching have not necessarily had any special training in intercultural communication (although an increasing number of ESL/EFL training programs are now requiring such training). If CETs are to be effective as peacemakers and teachers of intercultural sensitivity, it is therefore vitally important that they first make a sustained and serious effort to develop these skills themselves, not only so that these qualities will be modeled in their own lives, but also so that CETs can be more effective teachers of these skills. (We will return to this point again at the end of this chapter.)

Because the skills of intercultural communication are likely to be less familiar to CETs than are other teaching skills, this chapter will discuss the theoretical and practical aspects teaching more than has been done in previous chapters, and will also make a greater effort to suggest resources for further reading. It would not be possible to do justice to the entire field of intercultural communication in one brief chapter, so I have chosen to limit discussion below to three major problems which frequently lead to misunderstanding, misinterpretation, and even conflict in intercultural interactions, and which I believe are especially important to address in English classes: (1) the sheer unfamiliarity of alien cultures, and the tendency to stereotype the unfamiliar; (2) ethnocentrism; i.e., the human tendency to judge people of other cultures on the basis of the norms of ones own culture; and (3) in- and out-groups; i.e., the tendency to view foreigners as outsiders. This chapter will consider the ways in which these problems make peaceful cross-cultural interaction more difficult, and discuss approaches CETs can take in English class toward dealing with these problems.

Stereotyping the Unfamiliar

As students in non-Western countries begin the task of trying to understand Western culture, the first problem they are confronted with is its sheer unfamiliarity. This is not to say that students know nothing about the West. In fact, as a result of films, TV programs, and a variety of other Western media products, students in most host countries will know much more about the West than CETs initially know of the host country. However, such exposure to Western culture is generally rather superficial—how typical is the average Hollywood film of daily life in the United States? While it may signal to students that Western culture is in many ways different from their own, it generally does not provide a very detailed or accurate understanding of those differences. In fact, the primary results of such exposure are often stereotypes and overgeneralizations that are marginally accurate at best.

This problem, of course, is not unique to students of English. As Milton Bennett suggests, any person's initial understanding of another culture tends to be an oversimplified picture, painted in broad strokes in primary colors—or perhaps just in black and white. There is always a temptation to think of foreigners in terms of broad generalizations and stereotypes such as "Japanese are polite," "British are formal," and so forth.[5] Such generalizations are a natural and even inevitable part of thinking and talking about other cultures, and it is exceedingly difficult to talk about culture without making use of them.[6] After all, a culture is defined by those things a group shares in common, and many generalizations do have a degree of validity. (It is also simply more efficient in conversation to use generalizations than to qualify every statement with a mass of specific details and exceptions.) However, as students interact with individual people from other cultures—or even read books or articles written by people from other countries—this tendency to think about other cultures in broad generalizations also creates problems.

One problem with such generalizations and stereotypes is their inevitable inaccuracy. Cultures are very complex and true understanding is rarely if ever found in a few broad generalizations. Likewise, individuals tend to be complex, and it is a rare person who does not differ in some ways from what would be considered typical in his or her culture. A student who has a stereotyped understanding of a given foreign culture, and views all members of that culture as two-dimensional beings stamped from the same mold, is bound to frequently be very wide of the mark.

A second problem is that the tendency to overgeneralize and stereotype is fertile soil for the growth of prejudice. As we will see below, when encountering outsiders, i.e., people of different cultural backgrounds, people tend to be more harsh and negative in their judgments than they would be toward members of their own group. To make matters worse, when people encounter an outsider who behaves in a way they consider undesirable, they tend to attribute the problem to characteristics of the outsider's group and generalize that negative behavior to the rest of the group. In other words, they quickly move from individual judgments like "That Russian isn't very friendly" to more generalized sweeping judgments like "(All) Russians aren't very friendly." (When interacting with people of their own group background, people are more likely to find personal or situational explanations for the negative behavior—i.e., "Ivan isn't a very friendly person" or "Ivan probably didn't get enough sleep last night.)[7]

A third and more subtle danger, however, arises from the fact that stereotypes and generalizations can have a placebo effect, deluding students into believing that they already have the key to understanding another culture, and tempting them to prematurely abandon efforts to learn. Why should students bother to learn more if they already know that all English people are very polite and formal, or that all Americans base relationships on money? The problem created by this placebo effect is that students may plateau at a superficial level in their understanding of the West—or of any other alien culture—and not build the kind of realistic and detailed view that can serve as an effective counterweight to prejudice and racism. (Stereotypes can be overly positive as well as overly negative, but even unrealistically rosy views of other cultures are dangerous because they set people up for disillusionment.)

One obvious way CETs can address this problem in English lessons is by presenting information on Western culture through talks, readings, and other kinds of activities. While it is well beyond the range of any course to provide a comprehensive introduction to the culture of the West or even one English-speaking country, inclusion of information about selected aspects of Western culture generally makes English language courses more fun and interesting, and gives students a chance to know more about another culture. However, teaching information about Western culture can have a value that goes far beyond the inherent value of whatever discrete points of information are taught in a lesson about social problems in the United States, education in Britain, the history of Canada, or whatever. Culture lessons are an opportunity for CETs to present students with a more complex and realistic picture of aspects of Western culture, a richer fleshed-out picture that not only enhances students' understanding of particular aspects of the culture but also serves as a warning of the inaccuracy and danger of stereotypes and overly simple generalizations. A good culture lesson should leave students with the feeling that they have not only deepened their understanding of a foreign culture, but also that there is still much more for them to learn.

Lessons on Western cultures should help students see how much depth and complexity underlie a culture, and how much danger lurks in the temptation to make quick, facile generalizations. So CETs need to teach about culture in ways that will develop students' level of understanding from simple generalizations toward a more complex and sophisticated picture.

One strategy for doing this involves giving culture talks or readings that present students with a "rich" picture of Western culture which is more detailed and complex than their previous understanding. Consider, for example, the issue of how the elderly are treated in the United States. In my experience, in East Asia it is not uncommon for students to have the idea that young people in the United States do not care for the elderly, and that old parents are consigned to nursing homes when they reach the point where they can no longer take care of themselves. Needless to say, there is some truth underlying this generalization, but it is also grossly oversimplified. So, in order to present a richer view of this issue, a CET giving a talk on this topic might make some of the following points: It is true that the level of responsibility American children feel toward old parents is relatively low, at least compared to most Asian countries, and that many older Americans do live in nursing homes. However, there is a great deal of variation in the degree to which Americans care for their parents in old age, and many Americans interact with older parents a great deal. (Asian students are often surprised to discover that in the United States older parents sometimes *do* live with their children.) When older Americans do not live with their children, it is often in part because the parents don't want to be a "burden" on their children. Because the American emphasis on self-reliance, it is a point of pride for many older Americans to live independently and take care of themselves as long as is humanly possible. If and when older Americans do go into institutions for the elderly, there is also a great deal of variety in the kinds of establishments to which they go. Many retirement communities are quite different from students' impressions of the typical nursing home.

A talk that presents this kind of detail above can help students differentiate the broad categories through which they view American culture and help them generate more detailed categories which allow for more precise understanding. For example, it may help them discover that the broad category of "nursing home" should actually include a number of rather different kinds of institutions. It also helps students see that not all Americans are the same—and that it is dangerous to make assumptions as to how any individual American relates to his or her elderly parents. The point of such a talk is not to burden students with a level of detail that will overwhelm and confuse them, but rather to move them one or two steps further in their understanding of a foreign culture, and to suggest that there are many more such steps to be taken.[8]

A second strategy, which I call the "generalization + exception" strategy, is less a specific method than a useful habit which should come into play whenever CETs talk about culture. It is virtually impossible to talk about culture without resorting to generalizations. But teachers can prevent students from getting the false impression that generalizations adequately sum up a culture if they also make it a habit to mention exceptions to whatever generalizations they make. For example, when teachers are talking about the relative accent uniformity of English in the United States (compared to the more pronounced local differences in parts of the United Kingdom), they might also point out that there are communities in the United States where markedly different dialects of English are spoken—and even areas where the dominant language is Spanish. The exception serves to remind students that the generalization is only partly true, and it suggests the more complex nature of the picture underlying the generalization.

A similar strategy involves habitually specifying the degree to which any particular generalization is true. Consider the following three generalizations about Americans:

1. Americans drive cars.
2. Americans like rock and roll.
3. Americans are rich.

All three of these generalizations are true to some extent, but the degree of truth in each varies considerably. Generalization 1 is probably the most true; although not all Americans can or do drive, most Americans drive at least occasionally. Generalization 2 would be true for many Americans, but only for a limited percentage (and age bracket) of the United States population. Generalization 3 contains an element of truth, but is more problematic because the notion of "rich" is relative. This generalization is more valid in the context of a poor host country than it would in a relatively wealthy nation like Japan. The point here is these generalizations are more accurate and less misleading if they are properly qualified. (#1 would be better stated as "The great majority of Americans drive"; #2 as "Many young and middle-aged Americans like rock and roll," and so forth.)

Sometimes the effort CETs make to point out exceptions and qualify generalizations will go for naught. Students will only retain the gist of a generalization and quickly delete any qualifying details from their memories. However, by persistently reminding students that generalizations are only a rough approximation of the truth, and encouraging students toward a better and more detailed understanding, CETs can help students develop the habit of remaining open to learning more about other peoples and cultures. While encouraging students to avoid overgeneralizations and stereotypes will not in and of itself ensure that their relations with people of other cultures are harmonious, it is an important step. To the extent that students are cautious about making broad generalizations on the basis of little evidence, and see the importance of constantly being open to learning more about other cultures, they are less likely to fall back on stereotypes which are inaccurate, misleading, and often prejudicial.[9]

Perception, Ethnocentrism, and Empathy

A second major source of difficulty in intercultural interaction—in fact, possibly the single most serious source[10]—is ethnocentrism. Ethnocentrism can be defined as the tendency to view other cultures from the perspective of one's own culture, and to use the norms of one's own culture to judge the behavior of people from other cultures. This tendency is quite natural because, growing up in a given culture, students quite naturally learn to view the world from the perspective of that culture. In fact, the process of learning about one's culture and learning about the world in general are largely indistinguishable. As children learn what kind of behavior is polite and what behavior is rude, they generally come to understand these rules as universal norms rather than as culturally conditioned assumptions which will differ from one culture to another. For example, Americans don't think of prohibitions against spitting on the floor or belching after a meal as American customs. They think of these as rules of polite behavior that should be obvious to all of humankind. Likewise, in many Middle Eastern countries it is assumed that it is only natural and right that women should expose as little as possible of their bodies to public view.

As natural as ethnocentrism is, it is also highly problematic because it often leads students to interpret the words and actions of foreigners inaccurately, i.e., to understand what foreigners do and say in ways that are quite different from the ways those foreigners would understand their own actions. Take, for example, an incident in which a young Chinese woman tried to help an older Canadian man with his luggage. The Canadian rather quickly became annoyed at the Chinese woman's persistent efforts because he saw them as an indication that the Chinese woman thought he was too old to take care of himself. Meanwhile, the Chinese woman felt that she was only doing what younger people should always do for older people, and couldn't see why he did not appreciate her polite efforts to help. In this incident, both participants interpreted each other's behavior on the basis of their own cultural norms and the result was not only misunderstanding but also bad feelings on both sides.

Note that the problem created by ethnocentrism is not that it prevents students from being able to make sense of foreigners. In fact, students would have fewer problems in intercultural encounters if they treated any puzzling behavior on the part of foreigners as incomprehensible and withheld judgment until they learned more. The greater problem is that frequently students will *misunderstand* a foreigner's behavior, in other words, that they will think they have correctly interpreted that behavior when in fact they have not. Much in the way that stereotypes can function as placebos, lulling students into the belief that they understand more than they really do, ethnocentrism provides a familiar (but flawed) problem-solving mechanism which allows students to believe that they have correctly interpreted the actions and behaviors of a foreigner when their interpretation may actually be totally off the mark. This misinterpretation not only results in inaccurate interpretation and misunderstanding, but also closes the door to further learning. As William Gundykunst and Young Yun Kim note, once a person has found a "relevant and reasonable interpretation" of a foreigner's behavior, that person is likely to cease looking for alternative—and better informed—understandings.[11]

To make matters worse, when students use their own cultural norms as a basis for judging people from other cultures, this tends to prejudice them against behavior which is different from their own. As noted above, what people believe about what is right/wrong or good/bad depends heavily on the norms of their own culture. Thus, as students encounter foreigners—or even foreign films and books—they are tempted to judge anything which differs from their own cultural norms as, at least, abnormal and strange. This places foreign people and behaviors at a distinct disadvantage, and often leads students to judge other cultures as inferior.

The way in which ethnocentrism is closely interwoven with the process by which students interpret and judge the behavior of people from other cultures means that if CETs are to teach students less ethnocentric approaches to intercultural understanding, they need to address both ethnocentrism and the interpretation process itself. Three important goals toward which CETs should teach are:

- Raising students' awareness of the process by which they interpret and judge the behavior of foreigners, whether these be individual foreigners students actually meet or depictions of foreigners which students encounter in foreign books, articles, and films. The interpretation process usually operates more or less automatically, barely at the fringes of conscious thought, and tends to be so fast and automatic that people are not always consciously aware that they are engaging in it.[12] Consequently, the first step toward gaining control of this process is enhancing students' awareness of it and encouraging them to take conscious control of it rather than continuing to let it run on automatic pilot.

- Teaching students to be more thoughtful and careful in the process of interpretation, slowing the process down, or suspending it altogether. It is generally agreed by scholars of intercultural communication that training methods should encourage students to suspend or delay judgment so that they do not judge a situation without an adequate understanding of it.[13] Of course, there are situations in which students must react quickly to a foreigner whose behavior seems threatening or harmful, and in such situations they may not have the luxury of suspending judgment. However, in many intercultural encounters it is possible to delay judgment at least briefly, and after an encounter students always have the option of looking back at it and trying to understand it better. Students should also learn to view their interpretations of foreigners' behavior as lightly held "working hypotheses" rather than as final verdicts. If students develop the habit of seeing their judgments as preliminary theories to be reexamined and refined as new information becomes available, they are less likely to fall into the trap of having their understanding controlled by premature judgments. They are also more likely to be on the lookout for more information even after encounters are over, hence more likely to learn from experience.

• As teachers of cultural sensitivity, it is important for CETs to develop their students' ability to interpret other cultures with a greater degree of empathy. As Milton Bennet argues, essentially this means developing students' ability "to experience some aspect of reality differently from what is 'given' by one's own culture. . . . Empathy . . . describes an attempt to understand by imagining or comprehending the other's perspective."[14] CETs need to find ways to encourage students to try to understand other cultures from within their own frame of reference, to see these cultures from inside. Needless to say, students who have had little experience of a foreign culture will not suddenly be able to enter the worldview of that culture just because a teacher requests it, but they can learn to imaginatively seek different ways of viewing particular behaviors or situations, thus opening themselves up to interpretations other than those suggested naturally by their own cultural framework.

The goals suggested above are not easy to reach, particularly in a classroom setting, and they most certainly cannot be attained solely through classroom lectures. Ethnocentrism is an attitude which people begin learning at a very young age, and is therefore deeply rooted not only in students' minds but also in their emotions.[15] Talks directed at students' understanding may have limited impact on the deeper levels of their minds where attitudes such as ethnocentrism reside (especially if the talks are given in English to students with marginal listening skills, and laden with theoretical terms like "ethnocentrism"). A more effective approach is through classroom activities which engage students actively in the process of interpreting behavior which seems strange or foreign to them, and encouraging students to view that behavior from perspectives they might otherwise not consider. Professionals in the field of cross-cultural communication training have long made use of a number of specific activities which help students become more aware of the interpretation process and learn to see beyond ethnocentric perspectives, two of which are described below:

Critical incident exercises: These are exercises in which students hear or read a story about an encounter between people of two different cultures, generally an encounter in which there is some kind of problem or misunderstanding, and then discuss its interpretation. Consider a simple example. First students are presented with a little story like the following:

> (In China) Wang Li is riding in the same train compartment as a Canadian tourist and strikes up a conversation in order to practice her English. The Canadian seems willing to chat, so Wang Li starts asking him questions about his family and his job. As Wang Li continues to ask questions, the Canadian seems less and less willing to respond, and finally he gets up, says he wants to switch to a compartment where the air is better, and leaves.

Students are asked to discuss the incident and try to come to an understanding of what happened and why. (In this case, it may be that the Canadian was offended because Wang Li started asking overly personal questions about topics such as his marital status or salary, but it might also be that the Canadian got tired of practicing English with Wang Li, that he didn't really want to talk to anyone in the first place, or that he genuinely found the compartment too stuffy.) Critical incident exercises are usually open-ended in the sense that no "correct answer" is provided, although during or after discussion teachers often provide insight based on their cultural knowledge.

Critical incident exercises are especially good for helping students become more aware of the interpretation process, and by encouraging students to consider specific situations in more detail they also teach students to be more careful in the way they interpret intercultural encounters. Critical incident exercises are also useful in moving students beyond ethnocentric perspectives toward consideration of a broader range of alternative interpretations. However, the exercises in and of themselves do not contain a mechanism which ensures that this will happen. Students' will only see a broader range of alternatives if they themselves generate these alternatives or if the teacher suggests them.[16]

Intercultural sensitizer (ICS) exercises: Like critical incidents, intercultural sensitizer exercises begin with students listening to or reading a brief story describing a problematic encounter with a foreigner, and then discussing and interpreting the encounter. However, intercultural sensitizers differ from critical incident exercises in that they are not open-ended. Instead, students are presented with several ready-made possible interpretations of the encounter (usually four), and then asked to pick the interpretation *which they believe people of the foreigner's culture would pick.* This last point is very important because it shifts the focus of the exercise from the question "What is the right interpretation?" to the question: "How would people from the foreigners' culture view this incident?" After discussing the options, students then check the answer key to see which is the right answer.[17]

The great strength of this method is that it forces students to try to see things from the perspective of another culture. This is very helpful in encouraging them to move beyond their natural ethnocentric perspectives. By focusing the attention of students on issues of interpretation, intercultural sensitizers also raise students' awareness of the interpretation process. Failure to select correct answers should also alert students to the dangers of leaping to conclusions.

Even if a CET does not have time or opportunity to use exercises specifically designed to build empathy in cross-cultural interaction, there is generally ample opportunity to address the issue in the normal course of English study. Students are often exposed to examples of Western or foreign behavior through dialogues, stories, or other readings in their English language textbooks, or through foreign films and television programs. Undoubtedly, some of this behavior will seem unfamiliar and strange to students, and each time this happens, CETs have an opportunity to challenge students to consider why Westerners (foreigners) think and behave as they do, and to challenge students to look beyond obvious, instinctive, and ethnocentric interpretations and to consider other possible explanations.

No matter whether students are responding to examples of foreign behavior from a book, to imagined situations which the teacher creates for them, or to real encounters that they have had with Westerners or other foreigners, one key to increasing their degree of empathy is to ask them to place themselves in the shoes of the "other" and try to see the encounter as the other might have seen it. As noted above, the primary goal is not so much to have students find the "right" answer as it is to get them into the habit of using their imaginations to look beyond obvious (and often ethnocentric) interpretations. This habit will not necessarily always lead to more peaceful interaction between people of different cultures because it is quite possible that even when students correctly interpret the intentions of foreigners they will still not like what they see. However, if students learn to be careful about how they interpret the behavior of foreigners, there is less chance of conflict that arises from misunderstanding. Also, if students learn to achieve a degree of empathy in the ways in which they understand people of other cultures, there is a greater chance that they will judge them less harshly. In fact, it may be that it is virtually essential for those who would live out the Christian mandate to love others as you love yourself to learn to consciously strive to place themselves in the shoes of the other and see the world from the other's perspective.

In-groups, Out-groups, Self-interest, and the Benefit of the Doubt

A third problem which negatively impacts intercultural interaction is the universal tendency to categorize other people into in-groups and out-groups—"us" and "them"—and to treat members of one's in-group better than those of one's out-group.[18] At the root of this distinction no doubt lies the basic human tendency to love oneself more than others, but most people are not so self-centered that they have no concern for anyone other than themselves. Rather, they have a larger or smaller in-group consisting of people toward whom they have relatively positive feelings and a relatively strong sense of responsibility. (In fact, it could be argued that the process by which children are socialized is largely one of teaching them to broaden their in-group circle from a group consisting of one person—me—to gradually larger groupings such as "my family," "my clan," "my gang," "my town," "my company," and "my country.") However, the existence of the in-group assumes the existence of an out-group—"them"— consisting of people toward whom one feels less responsibility and has less positive feelings; in other words, people whose rights and needs are not as important as "ours." The problem this creates for CETs who wish to promote intercultural sensitivity and harmonious intercultural interaction is that few people have an in-group circle so large that it encompasses people of other cultures, and most people are predisposed to give foreigners less benefit of the doubt than they would give to other people of their own culture.

If, as suggested in the previous section, ethnocentrism is the single major source of problems in intercultural interactions, this would suggest that the core problem in such interactions is one of perspective and understanding, and that training should focus primarily on helping students better understand foreigners. While I would agree that much difficulty in intercultural communication is caused by misunderstanding and ethnocentrism, I suspect that self-centeredness, a trait which underlies the in-group/out-group issue above, is equally if not more important. To put the issue in more traditional Christian terms, people are sinners who tend to love themselves more than they love others, concerned primarily with their own interests, and they are often willing to do what is necessary to ensure that their interests prevail over those of other people. This results in conflict as "we" promote our well-being in competition with "them."

Of course, self-interest can lead to conflict even between people of the same culture (or household, for that matter), but generally the naked self-interest of individuals cannot pass itself off as anything more admirable than selfishness. Perhaps the most insidious effect of the tendency to divide the world into in- and out-groups is that it gives people a standard which allows them to make a virtue of protecting and promoting the interests of their in-group—their friends, family, countrymen, and so forth—while in effect declaring much of the world a free-fire zone in which it is not morally necessary to put the interests of others above one's own. The in/out-group dynamic allows people to cloak a broader form of self-interest in a degree of moral legitimacy, and at times it can even masquerade as virtue (at least among the in-group which benefits from the behavior).[19] The boundary which separates one culture from another is an especially fragile fault line, and it is often along this line that the human race chooses to divide itself into "us" and "them." Self-interest is therefore a particularly potent adversary to any attempt to promote an ethic of peace in intercultural interaction.

When students view foreigners as members of an out-group, and have a negative bias in the way they interpret the behavior of foreigners, there are several undesirable consequences. One is that in actual encounters, negative interpretations of the behavior of foreigners will often turn into self-fulfilling prophecies; the student will assume the worst of the foreigner and respond to the foreigner negatively, and then the foreigner will have cause to respond to the student negatively. Another consequence is that students will often imagine bad intentions and grievances that aren't really there. As noted earlier, once a person arrives at what appears to be a reasonable interpretation of a situation, the tendency is to cease looking for alternative explanations, so negative conclusions based on imagination have a nasty tendency to turn into permanent evidence that foreigners are not to be trusted.

As teachers of intercultural communication, part of the task of CETs is therefore to encourage students to counterbalance this natural tendency toward negative assessment of foreigners and their behavior. My suggestion is that as students are engaged in trying to interpret examples of foreign behavior, whether these arise from something students see in a Western film or book or from a critical incident exercise such as those suggested above, the CETs' role is to make sure that students give due consideration to relatively generous interpretations of that behavior as well as to negative possibilities; in other words, to encourage students to consider giving the benefit of the doubt.

One specific in-class method for addressing this issue is essentially a variation on the critical incident exercises introduced above. As with critical incident exercises, teachers present students with a short story of a problematic encounter between a student and a foreigner. (For this kind of exercise to work well, the situations need to be ambiguous enough that there is more than one reasonable interpretation, hence no single "right answer.") Students are then instructed to brainstorm a wide range of possible interpretations of the incident, generating a set of possible interpretations which range from generous to condemnatory. It is in this explicit instruction to consider generous as well as negative interpretations of the incident that this type of exercise differs slightly from a traditional critical incident exercise, and the inclusion of this request forces students to consider interpretations of the situation which give the foreigner in the encounter the benefit of the doubt. CETs cannot and should not force students to adopt a generous interpretation of the foreigners behavior—this would subtly suggest to students that the most generous interpretation is also the most likely, which may well not be the case. However, merely by raising the question CETs call students' attention to the issue, and suggest that the choice of whether to give the benefit of the doubt or not is in and of itself an important decision in intercultural interaction.

A problem raised by any suggestion that CETs should encourage students to give foreigners the benefit of the doubt, especially in direct personal encounters (as opposed to "virtual" encounters through books and films) is that in real life giving the benefit of the doubt entails a degree of risk. In the world of the English classroom, the issue of risk may seem rather remote. After all, characters in English language textbooks generally treat each other nicely no matter what cultural background they are from. However, people in the real world are generally not so polite, cheerful, and good-willed, and when students interact with real foreigners face-to-face they need to be aware of the possibility that they may be laughed at, looked down on, cheated, and perhaps worse. It is within this sobering context that CETs need to place any suggestion to students that they should give foreigners the benefit of the doubt.

This raises the question: What right do CETs have to encourage students to do something other than pursue self-interest, particularly if such behavior may entail risk? After all, many English teachers would hesitate to recommend a course of action to students that could potentially result in their being taken advantage of. It would no doubt often be safer if students were to approach foreigners with a fair degree of suspicion. One possible argument is that a "benefit of the doubt" approach to dealing with foreigners has practical advantages and is the strategy which, despite its risks, is still best for students' interests. For one thing, students who tend to give the benefit of the doubt are less likely to fan misunderstanding and tension into conflict and bad feelings, and students who tend to interpret generously are also less likely to respond negatively to situations in ways that slam the door on increased understanding. A "benefit of the doubt" approach also helps students maintain a stronger sense of goodwill toward the other culture. Many intercultural encounters, perhaps the majority, forever remain ambiguous in the sense that students will never learn all the details of what happened and why, so their interpretation always remains a working hypothesis. People whose default directory leads them to interpret ambiguous encounters negatively will more rapidly build up a fund of "war stories" about the other culture and its people, and as these war stories are passed around, they can have a major negative impact on what people think and feel about other cultures.

However, as Christians CETs also have grounds for believing it is ultimately right and good to place the interests of others on an equal footing with one's own, and even to risk personal loss on the behalf of other people—no matter what their nationality or culture. While there are many points on which Christians disagree, there is no question that for Christians a self-interest standard is not acceptable. Christians are called to a standard of behavior which entails loving our neighbors as ourselves (Matt. 22:38; Luke 10:27), loving our enemies, and even praying for those who persecute us (Matt. 5:43-44). Put another way, Christians are called to have an in-group that encompasses the entire human race. Perhaps this is illustrated most clearly in the parable of the good Samaritan where, in response to the question "Who is my neighbor?" Jesus upholds the example of a Samaritan who treated a Jew—an outsider and traditional enemy—in the same way as he would have treated one of his own (Luke 10:30-37).

This Christian "other-focused" love standard is a very demanding one which runs against the deepest human instincts. It is also a standard that Christians often fail to live up to, and CETs need to remember this when among peoples who have been wronged by "the Christian West" or even perhaps by Christian missionaries. It is thus a standard CETs need to uphold with great humility. However, Christians have no choice but to believe that such a standard is what God would have all people use in their dealings with each other. CETs cannot and should not command students to adopt such a standard, nor can CETs suggest that giving the benefit of the doubt will necessarily be the most accurate interpretation of a given situation. However, if CETs take Christ's admonition to be peacemakers seriously, as they teach students intercultural communication skills they need to raise this issue of generosity in judging foreigners, and even recommend it to students. The suggestion of an "other-focused" standard of cross-cultural interaction sends an important message about how Christians believe the world should be. This is one area of English teaching in which Christian teachers may have a truly special calling.

Sensitivity in Culture Teaching

Just as there are some in the language-teaching profession who would question the justice of promoting greater use of English worldwide on the grounds that this constitutes linguistic imperialism, questions are sometimes raised about the teaching of Western culture in English classes on the grounds that this is a form of cultural imperialism. My own feeling is that CETs need not seriously entertain extreme forms of this position which suggest that English teachers should not teach Western culture at all—the advantages of adding an element of Western culture in English classes are simply too great. As Lamin Sanneh suggests, genuine exchange between cultures is a beneficial thing. While Westerners should be sensitive to the legacy of the past, this does not mean they should not share what their culture has to offer.[20] However, because of the legacy of the past, the issue of cultural imperialism is one that CETs cannot afford to ignore entirely. If CETs teach about their culture in a boosterish way that seems to suggest Western culture is better than others, they may wind up rubbing salt in the wounds of the past rather than healing them. Similarly, if CETs only function as apologists for the West, constantly refuting all charges against it and explaining why it is misunderstood, students will soon come to question CETs' objectivity, and perhaps also wonder whether CETs view the world from any standard higher than their own cultural norms.

One quality CETs need to strive for as they teach about Western culture is objectivity. If CETs genuinely believe in a godly standard by which all human cultures are judged, this needs to be reflected in the way they teach about their own culture. It is for this reason that it is so important that CETs learn to see their own culture objectively, rather than having a view which is strongly colored by in-group affection and loyalty. If a CET's presentation of her or his culture becomes patriotic (and perhaps defensive), it highlights the in/out-group distinction in the classroom, with CETs and students on opposite sides of the divide. What CETs should strive toward in the classroom is an atmosphere in which "we" (including both CETs and students) discuss Western culture, the host culture, and human culture in general as objectively and fairly as possible. As Miroslav Volf argues: "Christians can never first of all be Asians or Americans, Croatians, Russians or Tutsis, and then Christians. At the very core of the Christian identity lies an all-encompassing change of loyalty, from a given culture with its goals to the God of all cultures."[21]

It is very difficult to be objective about one's own culture. CETs are no more immune to ethnocentrism and the in/out-group dynamic than anyone else. However, with discipline, it is possible to address issues of culture in ways which ensure a degree of balance and at least some degree of impartiality. One useful strategy involves consistently pointing out both advantages and disadvantages, good and bad, strong and weak points of whatever aspects of culture are under discussion. For example, a Canadian teacher talking about the bilingual, multi-cultural nature of Canada should point out the advantages of such pluralism, but also be honest about some of the difficulties involved (for example, those between French- and English-speaking Canadians). Likewise an American teaching students about the fine highway system in the United States should also note the role this system has played in the decline of public transportation, and a consequent increase in pollution from private cars.

It is rare for any good feature of a culture not to have its dark side or disadvantages, and even the most unappealing characteristic of a culture is generally not without some redeeming qualities or at least a logical explanation. If CETs consistently seek for and point out both sides of the story, their presentation of cultural issues will not only seem more fair and objective, but also actually be more balanced. It may seem somewhat artificial to always point out both a good and bad point of every feature of culture, and there may be times when CETs have to strain to find both a positive and negative quality in a particular point of culture. However, the very consistency of this approach is important in drilling home the habit of seeing all cultures as having both good and bad sides, and it helps send the message that CETs respect all human cultures.[22]

A second quality which CETs should strive for in their culture teaching is sensitivity. In many nations either the colonial past or a history of conflict with the West has left many people with raw feelings toward the West. These feelings and the beliefs that underlie them may not always be entirely fair. However, whether fair or not, these feelings are often powerful, and CETs need to take them into account when teaching about Western culture if unpleasant conflict in class is to be avoided. This involves knowing which issues to treat gently and which issues to avoid entirely. One reason it is so important for CETs to have a good knowledge of their host culture is precisely so that they know where the landmines are buried and how lightly they need to tread in order to avoid setting them off.

Sensitivity does not mean that CETs always need to agree with students' views of the West. Sometimes the views CETs encounter will be unfairly negative, and it is part of their duty as teachers to help students toward a fairer and more empathetic understanding. However, CETs need to do this with a great deal of patience and gentleness, particularly with issues where grievances run deep. CETs may need to carefully consider the question of how much they can challenge a particular set of views without alienating a group of students entirely. Sensitivity in this case can mean finding a compromise in which CETs sometimes let issues go, sometimes suggest an alternative point of view, and occasionally take a stronger stance.

Sensitivity also requires a considerable degree of humility on the part of CETs. One of the charges most often leveled at Western missionaries, both past and present, has been the accusation that Western Christians consider themselves and their culture to be superior. Therefore, CETs may at times need to bend over backward a little in an attempt to ensure that they do not make this problem any worse. It is not desirable for CETs to go to the opposite extreme, becoming critical of everything in their own culture, but it is often diplomatically wise to make a special point of those aspects of the host culture from which the West can learn and to be scrupulously fair in willingness to admit failings where they exist in Western culture. (Given the human instinct toward generosity with one's own culture and a negative evaluation of other cultures, a conscious attempt to lean a little in the other direction will probably produce a roughly fair balance rather than excessive identification with the host culture.)

An additional way that CETs can ensure a degree of sensitivity in teaching culture is by using lessons based on cultural issues as an opportunity to learn more about the host culture. There is no better way for students to engage in genuinely communicative use of English in class than to practice English by explaining their own culture to the teacher, particularly if the teacher is genuinely interested in learning.[23] Furthermore, by making culture lessons exchanges rather than a one-sided presentation on the part of the teacher, CETs can make such lessons more interesting and also reinforce the message that they are willing to learn about the host culture.

Finally, we need to remember that CETs need to be students and practitioners of cultural sensitivity as well as teachers of it. As noted in the introduction to this chapter, CETs do not necessarily have much more expertise in this area than their students do, and while it is still an important area for CETs to teach, they need to be careful not to give students the impression that they believe themselves to be superior in their level of cultural sensitivity. The impression that CETs should create is rather that they and students are seekers together on a road toward greater intercultural sensitivity and understanding. However, in the kind of limelight existence many CETs enjoy, this impression won't last long unless it is backed up by genuine efforts on the part of CETs to learn the host culture and to learn to interact empathetically with its people. It is when students see CETs actually trudging along the road toward greater intercultural sensitivity and understanding that students are most likely to fall in willingly alongside.

8

English Teachers as Bridges Between Churches

Not long ago, a British couple was preparing to return to their home country after several years of service as English teachers in China. During their years in China, they had participated in the life of a local Chinese church and developed an especially close relationship to that community. As they were paying their farewell visit to the congregation and saying good-bye to the pastor, they asked what, if anything, they could do for the church after returning home. The pastor's request was simple and straightforward: Please tell people in your country about the church here in China, tell them what you have seen and experienced here.

This brief anecdote suggests a final important role that CETs can and should play, that of "interpreters" who participate in and learn about the experience of the Christian church in their host country, and share what they learn with churches at home. Christians from different cultures need to share experiences and insights with each other, and one of the best ways for this to happen is through Christians from one culture who go live with Christians of another culture long enough to gain a good understanding of their host church and to serve as interpreters of that church's experience to the home church. The role CETs can play in this process is special because CETs often work in nations where there is little Western Christian presence, and they have an opportunity to participate in and learn about churches which are not well understood in the West. These are also often churches whose past relations with Western Christianity have been troubled in various ways. CETs have a unique opportunity to work toward reconciliation by building bridges of fellowship and understanding between Christian communities which may not have especially close or cordial relations with each other.

In this chapter we will consider in more detail the challenges CETs face in this process of keeping Christian communities in different parts of the world linked with each other. In particular, we will focus on issues related to CETs' participation in the life of churches in their host countries, and to the sharing of what they learn with churches back home. However, we will begin with an even more basic question: Why is it important for Christian churches of different cultural and faith traditions to be in contact with each other at all? To be more specific, why is it important for Western churches to build or maintain relationships with other churches in other countries through the sending of Western mission personnel?

The Need for Churches to Be in Contact

There may seem to be little need to argue that it is important for churches of different traditions and national backgrounds to build and maintain contact with each other, or to argue that the exchange of mission personnel should play a major role in this process. However, I feel that it is worth devoting attention to this issue because within Western churches at both the conservative and liberal ends of the theological spectrum there are dynamics which work against the sending of mission personnel abroad for this purpose.

Among churches toward the more evangelical end of the spectrum, it is sometimes assumed that evangelism is the primary and perhaps even exclusive call of missionaries. This assumption tends to direct Christians from these traditions toward work in places where Christian presence is minimal, thus decreasing the chances they will have contact with local

Christians of other traditions. Also, while many evangelical groups are very active in bridge building with Christians of other traditions, it is probably fair to say that Western Christians from conservative and evangelical backgrounds don't always give high priority to building and maintaining relationships with churches whose theological traditions are very different from their own. So when evangelical Western Christians encounter Christian groups in the host nation who they view as being theologically suspect—or perhaps just not sufficiently vital and oriented toward evangelism— the Western Christians sometimes make little effort to build bridges to these local Christians.

For Western churches toward the more mainline and/or liberal end of the spectrum, the danger is somewhat different. Among these churches there is generally a relatively high level of commitment to establishing and maintaining relations with churches in different countries. Mission personnel sent abroad by these churches are more likely to have some kind of tie to a Christian church in the host country, and are more likely to see the nurturing of such relations as part of their mission role. However, among these churches there is also a stronger sense that Western mission efforts of the past, especially evangelistic efforts, smacked too much of cultural imperialism. So the general level of enthusiasm and support for missions is somewhat lower than in evangelical churches and there is generally an effort to avoid any mission initiatives which seem unilateral. Also, while most of these churches still maintain substantial mission programs, their programs tend to be smaller (in relative terms) than those of evangelical churches, and they simply don't send as many people abroad, especially for longer-terms of service.

For these very different reasons, at either end of the theological spectrum, there is the danger that Western churches may not give high enough priority to the sending of Western Christians abroad as a channel for contact between their home churches and churches in the host country, with the result that too few Western Christians will have a deep understanding of the life of the church in other nations and cultures. For this reason it is worth reemphasizing a number of important reasons why churches of different regions and traditions should strive to be in contact with each other, and why Western churches should make use of their mission personnel as bridges in this way:

- At the most practical level, there is the need for different churches to assist and support each other both materially and spiritually through prayer and encouragement. We see examples of this kind of support between churches even in the earliest years of Christian church history; for example when the church in Antioch gathered money and sent it to Jerusalem in order to aid Christians there through the hardships of a famine (Acts 11:29-30; see also Rom. 1:8-13).

It is possible for Western churches to materially and spiritually support churches elsewhere without sending personnel, but the presence of Western Christians can do much to facilitate the flow of information from host churches abroad to churches in the West, as well as vice versa. This enables Christians to pray in a more informed way for each others' needs, respond with material gifts when necessary, and be encouraged by hearing about how God is working in other parts of the church. In one sense, the missionary functions as an on-the-spot reporter who not only has good access to information, but also knows the host country and church well enough to place that information in perspective and present it in a balanced and informed manner. This role can be especially helpful in the case of host churches which are little known in the West, or host churches about which such information as is available in the West tends to be inaccurate. Western churches are often eager to assist Christians in other parts of the world, and have considerable resources for doing so, but if such assistance is not based on a good understanding of the local situation, it may turn out to be more well intended than useful.

- Another reason for churches to be in communication with each other is that such interaction is one important way of bearing witness to the essential unity of the church. Despite God's desire that all Christians be one church and one body, a point which Paul argues at some length in 1 Corinthians, the Christian church is obviously fragmented into a bewildering variety of groups that seem to have so little in common with each other that it is not hard to understand why many people outside the faith assume that different Christian traditions are entirely distinct and different religions.[1] Given that this situation is not likely to change dramatically in our lifetimes—new splits and divisions seem to occur almost as fast as groups come together—the least that Christians of different traditions can do to demonstrate the commonality of their faith to the world is interact with each other.

Personnel sent from one church to another are a powerful symbol of the unity of the Christian church, what David Bosch calls "living symbols of the universality of the church . . . a living embodiment of mutual solidarity and partnership."[2] Needless to say, this exchange of personnel should not be one-sided, and it is beneficial for Western churches to receive Christians from other churches in other parts of the world. However, it is equally important for Western Christians to be sent abroad.

• A third reason follows closely on the second. Sadly, disunity within the Christian faith is not simply a matter of different but mutually respecting traditions. It is often one of conflicts and divisions both ancient and modern. Between many churches there needs to be a process of reconciliation and healing before there can be meaningful fellowship, let alone any movement toward unity. As argued earlier, this is particularly true of relationships between Western churches and those in many other parts of the world. Therefore, another reason Western churches should continue to send mission personnel to other countries is that this aids in a process of reconciliation that we have considered at various points through this book. In places where there is resentment toward the West and toward Western Christians because of real or imagined grievances of the past, the presence of Western Christians who serve and live in ways that bring credit to the churches which send them can be an important avenue for healing wounds of the past. Needless to say, good can also be done by Western churches through programs that provide funds and material aid, but the physical presence of Western missionaries helps build relationships in a way that other forms of church activity cannot.

• There is a fourth, possibly less obvious, reason that different churches need to be in communion with each other, having to do with what Christians the world over can learn from each other as we strive toward an understanding of God and how he calls us to live out our faith. To borrow an analogy from agriculture, as cross-fertilization helps plant populations maintain their health, Christian communities need to interact, to share ideas and experiences, in order that they do not stagnate. As David Bosch argues: "[A]ll theologies, including those in the West, need one another; they influence, challenge, enrich, and invigorate each other. . . ."[3] This effect occurs because each particular Christian community has a unique gift to bring to the whole. As Paul Hiebert points out: "Not only are all cultures capable of expressing the heart of the gospel, but each also brings to light certain salient features of the gospel that have remained less visible or even hidden in other cultures. Churches in different cultures can help us understand the many-sided wisdom of God, thereby serving as channels for understanding different facets of divine revelation, truths that a theology tied to one particular culture can easily overlook."[4]

One particular way in which the experience of different Christian communities can be of special benefit to others is through helping them see the ways in which culture and Christian faith become intermixed and often confused with each other. For example, for Christians who grow up always having Christmas trees and evergreen boughs strewn about at Christmas, or with the assumption that church and state should be separate, it is easy simply to assume that these are natural and even inevitable aspects of the Christian faith, and never to question them—or even really notice them.

However, for the health of our faith Christians need to be aware of and even prune away the cultural buildup and "elements of syncretism" in our faith.[5] In order to do this we need to get outside of our own cultural perspective and look at Christianity from another cultural viewpoint. It is often only when we experience the Christian faith in another culture (where perhaps they have no Christmas trees or do not pursue a strict policy of separation between church and state) that these and many other cultural assumptions are forcefully brought to our attention and we are stimulated to consider the degree to which they are an essential part of the Christian faith. Christian communities need to develop an understanding of Christianity in which cultural accretions are not confused with the essentials of the faith, and Christians of different cultural backgrounds can help each other see cultural assumptions more clearly. It is therefore important that Christian communities in different cultures interact with each other, each from our perspective and experience sharing our understanding of the gospel and shedding whatever light we have on the grand mystery of our faith.

It could be argued that the task mentioned above belongs in the domain of theologians, and no doubt to some degree it does. However, if this cross-fertilization is to affect the daily life of the church at all levels, rather than just its seminaries and national offices, there must be a steady flow of people from one church to another—people who can live in another country long enough to gain a genuine degree of understanding of its life and Christian experience. Of course, to some extent contact can be maintained through conferences and exchanges of delegations, and also through the many Christians from abroad who come to the West for study in secular and church institutions. In this process of mutual learning, the role played by Christians from non-Western churches and nations, articulating their experience and perspective to Western Christians, is very important.

However, in this process it is also important that Western Christians play a role, and it is not likely that Western churches will be able to maintain anything more than a superficial understanding of the Christian church in other cultures unless a substantial number of Western Christians have extended and in-depth experience in those churches.

The role CETs have to play in this process is special because the secular nature of their work and the worldwide demand for English combine to create opportunities for many CETs to live and work in countries where there are few other Western Christians. They thus often have opportunity for contact with Christian groups which otherwise don't often have Western visitors and may have little contact of any kind with Western churches—or other churches of any kind. Sometimes this lack of contact results from government policy or social disapproval which limit the contacts permissible. In other cases the problem is more that the churches themselves choose to keep a distance from churches of the West, either because of ancient rivalries or more recent conflicts. Sometimes the problem is just that the host country is relatively remote or off the beaten track. Whatever the case, CETs often have the opportunity to open windows onto a range of Christian experiences which might otherwise remain closed to most Western Christians.

Issues in Approaching the Local Church

Some CETs are sent to other countries as part of an ongoing relationship between home churches and churches in the host country and arrive in the host country with ready-made introductions which greatly facilitate their entry into the life of the church in the host country. However, more often than not, CETs go to the host country through an arrangement with a school rather than a church. They lack any natural introduction to Christians within the host country and arrive with little idea of what Christian churches in the host country are like or how to go about approaching them.

How CETs go about approaching a host church depends to a large extent on what kind of church it is. At the risk of over-simplification, I would suggest that from the perspective of a CET, these churches can be viewed as falling into a number of basic types:

- Ancient non-Western churches (such as the Coptic churches in Ethiopia, and Orthodox churches in Russia and much of Eastern Europe). These ancient churches play a dominant religious and cultural role in the lives of their countries, and have traditions which differ in many ways from those of Western Catholic or Protestant churches. Many of these churches would look at Western Christians, especially Protestants, as competitors more than as coreligionists.

- Ancient non-Western minority churches (such as Coptic churches in Egypt, Orthodox churches in the Middle East, and Syrian churches in India). These ancient churches survive in areas which are dominated by other religions, often Islam. They are often marginalized in the life of their countries, and may form a subculture which is more or less cut off from the mainstream of their country's cultural and religious life. As above, they may look on Western Christians as competitors.

- "Daughter" churches of Western mission efforts (such as Presbyterian churches in Korea and Taiwan, Anglican churches in Japan, and so forth). These are churches which were founded by Western missionaries and still identify to some degree with the tradition of those missionaries. Most are minority churches in the sense that they are in countries that are not predominantly Christian, but they may have a social role and prominence beyond their numerical size, especially if they run schools, hospitals, and other social welfare institutions. On the other hand, they may also be marginalized or even persecuted subgroups in their societies, sometimes because of their historical association with the West. Many of these churches still have organizational ties with their mother churches, either on a bilateral basis or through international bodies (such as, for example, the Lutheran World Federation or the World Council of

Reformed Churches), but they may have also made efforts to distance themselves from their Western past.

- Modern indigenous churches (such as the "Little Flock" churches in China or the many independent churches in Africa). These are churches which were not founded by Western missionaries, although their founders may have been indirectly inspired by the activity of Western missionaries and their theology may have borrowed significant elements from Western Christianity. Often these churches grew in some sense as a reaction to the work of Western missionaries, and are proud of the fact that their origins are not Western, although this does not necessarily mean that they are anti-Western. They may play a well-established and accepted role in the life of their countries, or they may be a persecuted minority.

- "Infant" churches. By this term I refer to small groups of Christians who are just beginning to form into Christian church bodies, often in areas where there is little other Christian presence. These churches may result from the efforts of local or Western evangelists, or of local people who have become Christian elsewhere and brought their new faith back home. As newly formed bodies, they may not yet have strong traditions or a well-defined sense of identity. Their relationship to the local society may not yet be clearly defined (if only because they are so new that they have not yet attracted much attention).

The summary above raises at least three issues relevant to CETs as they consider how to establish contact with a local church, or whether to do so at all:

- The first relates to whether or not it is in the best interests of the church to have CETs attend. In some countries the church is more tolerated than accepted, and it is only by keeping a low profile that the church avoids harassment or even persecution. The problem in these situations may be that the presence of a Western outsider would draw unwanted attention to the church. This is an especially important consideration in countries where Christian gatherings are culturally or legally proscribed, and where Christian gatherings are secret or very low profile. However, even in some countries where Christians are legally allowed to worship, official or popular suspicion makes their activities very sensitive, and it may be better for the church for CETs not to attend.[6]

- A second issue concerns whether or not CETs wish to be associated in the public mind with the local church. One reason CETs might wish to avoid such association is that "local" Christian churches in some host countries may actually be more closely associated with an outside group or nation than with the majority of the local population. This would be the case, for example, in some predominantly Muslim nations in Central Asia which were once part of the Soviet Union and therefore have communities of Russian Orthodox Christians.[7] In such churches Christians may be more concerned with maintaining a distance from local people than with making the church more open to them, and participation in such a church might have the effect of distancing CETs from the majority of the local population. While CETs might still choose to participate either for their own learning or spiritual growth—or perhaps in hopes of gently persuading local Christians to be more open to the rest of the local population—the cost of such association is something CETs should consider.

CETs may also have doubts about participation in a local church because of local beliefs and practices which differ considerably from those CETs are used to. Some of these differences can readily be dismissed as minor variations on a universal Christian theme, but others will be major differences which run directly against convictions deeply held by CETs, and which might cause CETs to doubt the efficacy of being identified with a given church. This is a genuine concern because all over the world (including in the West) there are many groups calling themselves Christian which have beliefs and practices that are of dubious orthodoxy or are downright heretical. Before joining such a group Christians need to think seriously about the implications for their own spiritual health as well as the message their participation in such groups sends to others.

However, CETs should also be cautious about deciding not to participate in a local Christian church on the grounds that it is imperfect in doctrine or practice. When CETs encounter practices in the host country church which are different from their own, their first impulse is often to assume that something is wrong with the faith or practice of host country Christians. CETs, like Christians from any and all backgrounds, are affected by ethnocentrism in the sense that all Christians are instinctively tempted to believe that our own form of Christian faith and practice is the best, and we see the syncretism and cultural accretions in the practice of other Christians more clearly than we see our own. (Consider the tolerance most Western Christians show toward pagan symbols such as evergreen trees at Christmas, or bunnies and colored eggs at Easter.)

It is actually at points where local Christian practice violates the expectations of Western Christians that there is the most potential for CETs to learn and grow toward a more universal and balanced understanding of the Christian faith. Christian practices and beliefs in other cultures which differ from CETs' own have the beneficial effect of challenging CETs' cultural assumptions about what is and is not proper Christian belief and practice, calling those assumptions to their attention and forcing them to be examined more carefully. Upon examination, CETs may decide that some of their assumptions about Christianity are more based in Western culture and tradition than in the faith itself; in other cases CETs may ultimately conclude that their original assumptions were correct and that it is the church in the host culture which needs to reflect more carefully on the validity of a particular belief or practice.

This latter judgment, however, is one CETs should make only after considerable thought, prayer, and effort to learn and understand. In fact, the question of whether or not exposure to the Christian faith in other cultures will help CETs in their own faith—and ultimately help their home churches—depends largely on how CETs process what they experience. If they judge prematurely, the effect of exposure to other traditions of Christianity will be to confirm prejudices and a sense of superiority. If, however, CETs are able to suspend their natural critical impulses, and make a sustained effort to learn and understand before passing judgment, the experience should be productive in the maturation of their faith.

- The third issue raised by our brief survey of host country churches concerns how open and welcoming CETs can expect local churches to be. In some countries, especially those where Christianity is a stigmatized minority faith, the Christian church has had a ghetto-like existence for centuries and is simply unaccustomed to welcoming outsiders. Often in such churches Christianity is viewed more as a cultural identity into which one is born than a faith which people can freely choose to enter or leave. Such a view would naturally not dispose a church community to be very open to outsiders. Even in countries where Christians are not a stigmatized minority, local Christians may simply not be accustomed to being joined by Western visitors—they don't know who these foreigners are, why they are there, or quite how to deal with them.

In other nations, Christians may be standoffish toward Western Christians because of mixed feelings local Christians have about Westerners and even Western Christians, perhaps as a result of a difficult historical legacy. As we saw in chapter 2, churches in many countries have had a checkered historical experience with Western Christians, with the result being that they may not always be inclined to welcome Western CETs with open arms. This is especially true when CETs are strangers who do not come as part of a church-to-church relationship or have not been introduced by someone the local church people know and trust.

My purpose in pointing out the possible reluctance which local churches might have toward accepting CETs into their midst is not to suggest that CETs should avoid these churches. In fact, it may be precisely these churches to which it is most important for CETs to go. However, CETs do need to go with the expectation that they may need to earn trust and acceptance. This is a process which may require considerable time and patience, but CETs should view the effort and sacrifice involved in this process as part of their mission of reconciliation. An important part of this task is the effort to learn more about the local church and understand it better, and it is to the practical problems involved in this process that we turn next.

Learning about the Local Church

Many CETs who have the opportunity to participate in a local church in the host country find that this is one of the most rewarding and meaningful aspects of their experience. Foremost among these rewards for many CETs are the relationships they build with Christians in the host country. However, many also experience a deepening and maturation of their own faith as a result of experiencing the Christian life from a different perspective that allows new insights into God's character.

The process of becoming part of a local church is often challenging, and there are a number of difficulties which should not be ignored. One of the most obvious of these for many CETs is the language barrier—CETs who don't speak the host language are cut off from both comprehension of worship and from much interaction with host country Christians, and this often makes attending worship discouraging. Another problem is that many CETs only serve in the host country for relatively short periods, and many have the frustrating experience of seeing their relationships with people in the local church blossom only during the final part of their stay.

However, the most basic issue may be one of intentionality. No matter how long CETs plan to stay in the host country, they will probably not develop a good understanding of the local church unless they see it as part of their role to become a knowledgeable interpreter of the experience of the host country church, and make a deliberate and diligent effort to learn as much as possible during whatever time they have. This task may demand considerable patience and effort. It is quite possible that even after several years in the host culture CETs will have only a limited understanding of the church. However, even CETs who do not become experts can still have something very valuable to offer to their home church communities if they take advantage of the opportunities they have in the host country to learn about its church.

Given the great variety of possible situations CETs may encounter in their efforts to learn about the host country church, such suggestions as I can make about the process are general at best, but may still throw a little light on the issue:

Regular attendance: One of the simplest but most effective ways for CETs to begin the process of becoming part of a local church community is through establishing the discipline of regular church attendance. This is not always easy in settings where CETs can't understand much of what goes on in church, or where they may feel awkward sitting in the middle of a group of people they don't know and seem to have little in common with. However, presence on a regular basis goes a long way toward demonstrating commitment and building trust.

Observation: Unless CETs stay in the host culture for a long time, or arrive with a knowledge of the local language, it is likely that their ability to understand worship services and interact with local Christians will be limited. In such situations, CETs should not underestimate the importance of simply being good observers. Often just by being present in church and observing, they can learn a great deal of value to share with Christians in their home country. Of course it is important that CETs be cautious about drawing broad conclusions on the basis of limited observations, and that they find ways to check the accuracy of whatever conclusions they reach. But there are many important things that can be learned and stated with confidence based on observation alone. When sharing with people at home the most powerful and credible witness often comes in the form of "I was there and this is what I saw."

Offering to be of service: Sometimes it is possible for CETs to assist with simple manual tasks (helping clean up after services, etc.) requiring little in the way of language skills. The idea of a Western teacher (guest) helping in such ways would be resisted in some cultures, but such service demonstrates the willingness of CETs to help at the same time that it demonstrates that they are willing to serve as well as to teach and lead.

Teaching roles: Given the nature of CETs' work, one obvious way for them to participate in a local church is through some kind of teaching role. The degree to which CETs can be of assistance to the local church through teaching, whether this means teaching English or teaching in specifically Christian areas, will vary greatly depending on the local situation and CETs' background, so it is difficult to make specific suggestions. However, there are two principles that will be of help in many situations. The first is that CETs who are new to the host culture should be cautious about assuming their readiness for roles that involve teaching Christian doctrine and practice. When talking about their own Christian faith and experience, CETs are on fairly safe ground, but it is quite another thing for CETs who know little of the local culture to teach local people how the gospel should be applied in their culture. As was argued in chapter 3, the process of "translating" the gospel in the host culture has generally begun long before the arrival of a CET, and it behooves newly arrived Western Christians to learn about how the gospel has already started taking root in the host culture before assuming a teaching role.

Secondly, there is much wisdom in the biblical principle of seating oneself at the end of the table and only taking a more honored seat if and when invited (Luke 14:8-11). Sometimes Western CETs approach a local church with the assumption that their proper role is as teachers and leaders, assuming that an inherent aspect of the missionary role is taking leadership and teaching roles in churches overseas, or perhaps even (subconsciously) that Westerners have a better understanding of Christianity than local Christians do.[8] In most situations, there is no harm in CETs taking a more passive role, participating in worship and waiting to see what else they might be able to do for the church, rather than entering the situation with a preset agenda. Willingness to be led, and to wait for invitations from local Christians, is in and of itself an important message of respect.

Explicit information gathering: As CETs become known in the church community, they might ask church leaders for more formal interviews so that they can gather material for interpretation letters to send to home churches. Needless to say, CETs need to be sensitive to the local situation, and such a request may be more problematic in some countries than in others. CETs may also create difficulties if they view such interviews as an opportunity for investigative reporting, uncovering the dirty linen of the church, or pushing their own agenda (prodding the church with questions about why they allow infant baptism, don't have women pastors, or whatever). However, in many countries Christian leaders and lay people will be willing to cooperate with CETs in this interpretation task as long as they sense that CETs are sympathetic, desire to hear and understand what they have to say, and will faithfully represent their voices to the CETs' audience.

The learner role: When CETs ask local Christians to teach them, it not only creates an opportunity for CETs to learn, but also shows respect for local Christians by placing them in the teacher role. CETs might begin with simple requests such as asking local Christians to teach them some hymns or prayers (the Lord's Prayer, for example) in the local language, or asking to study the Bible in the local language with someone from the church. As relationships develop, CETs then ask people to teach them more about the local church. (When a CET can find a language teacher within the church community, he or she has the opportunity to learn the host language, learn about the church, and build a relationship with someone in the church all at the same time.)

CETs should view this idea of taking a learner role in host churches as a part of their Christian witness, especially in cultures where the local church grew out of efforts of Western missionaries. By attending church as ordinary parishioners instead of church leaders, and by allowing themselves to be pastored and cared for by the local Christian community, CETs demonstrate respect for the maturity of the local church and "give face" to its leaders. Westerners participating in a local church in this way may even enhance the general regard in which the church and its leaders are held in the local community. More importantly, taking a learner role makes it plain that CETs have come to learn, not just to teach. This will go a long way toward disarming suspicions that Western Christians think they are superior.

Sharing with Churches at Home

It is vitally important that Western churches understand the experience of non-Western churches and Christians, not only for the spiritual health of Western churches, but also because of the influential role churches in the West, especially the United States, play in the life of the world's most powerful nations. Because of the influence, wealth, and resources of Western churches, they are in a position to have a considerable impact on Christian churches elsewhere in the world. The Western tendency toward international activism combines with the call of the gospel to make it virtually certain that Western churches will make such an impact. The question is whether this impact will be positive or negative, with the latter being a real possibility, and this in turn depends on how wisely Western churches exercise their influence.

One problem to which Western churches (and churches anywhere) are prone is ethnocentrism—the tendency to view God and his mission only from the perspective of one's own culture and experience. This often makes it difficult for Western Christians to discern what God's call might be in the context of a culture other than their own. A closely related problem is a sense of spiritual pride and superiority that too often makes Western Christians slow to listen to and learn from the experience of Christians from other backgrounds. While Western Christians have no monopoly on pride, this problem is especially difficult for Western Christians because the power of their churches and nations tends to feed a sense of superiority. Finally, as Western churches seek to engage in God's mission in any given host nation, their ability to discern that mission is hampered by a sheer lack of information about the host nation in question. The combined result of these problems is that in many nations Western attempts to engage in God's mission are more well-intentioned than well-informed.

While love can cover a multitude of sins, it should also compel Western churches to do all that is within their power to learn about other nations, about the church in other nations, and to ensure that the mission call they follow is God's rather than their own.

The role which CETs can play in this process is no doubt limited, but also significant, especially given that CETs often have firsthand experience of the church in nations and cultures which attract special attention from mission-oriented Western Christians but in which relatively few Western Christians have lived. In order to be effective in helping Western churches better understand the churches of their host countries, CETs need to do more than make an active effort to learn about the host country church. They also need to intentionally prepare for the task of sharing what they learn with Christians at home, a task which sometimes requires more perseverance and planning than CETs might expect. In some cases the problem is that some Christians at home just aren't very interested in the world beyond their own experience. Perhaps the most classic manifestation of this problem, familiar to many returnees from abroad, is the experience of being asked "How was Russia (Slovakia, Thailand, wherever)?" and then being expected to sum up several years of experience in one or two comments, preferably confined to 25 words or less. The problem here becomes one of generating interest and convincing people that there is something they can learn from the experience of other Christian communities.

There will also be people who have a stereotyped—and perhaps very negative—view of a CET's host culture, and are resistant to any information that contradicts or challenges their opinions. These attitudes are most often encountered by CETs returning from countries which have a history of adversarial relations with the CET's home country, or have had a great deal of negative exposure in the press. Here the problem becomes one of convincing listeners to modify their views.

A final problem is that people frequently have difficulty relating to any experience which seems very distant and foreign. They are interested and curious in a general way, but they do not know enough about the CET's host country to know what questions to ask. Much in the same way that the average person finds it difficult to make conversation with a mathematician about chaos theory. People who lack even basic knowledge about a foreign country or culture don't know where to begin asking about it. The challenge in this case is how to provide cues that will help people generate questions.

Of course, this is not the whole story. There will be many people who are interested in what CETs have to share, especially if they can present it in an interesting way that is easy for people to relate to. However, in order to be effective as interpreters it is generally necessary for CETs to give time and attention to devising strategies which will make it easier for people at home to digest what they have to share. Among such strategies are:

Early commitment to the interpretation task: The greatest problem many CETs face in the interpretation role is just that they don't take it seriously enough or devote enough time and effort to it. Quite naturally while CETs are in the host country much of their attention is devoted to teaching work, building relationships, learning the local language and culture, not to mention daily survival, so it is not unusual for

CETs to consider the issue of interpretation only when they need to write letters home, or even to let the interpretation issue wait until they actually return home. The first step is thus not only commitment to learning about the church in the host country, but also to reflecting on messages and experiences that would be valuable to communicate with Christians at home, gathering relevant information and material, and giving thought to how these messages could best be communicated. While CETs are in the host country, they should also give thought to building a collection of pictures, slides, videotapes, artifacts, and souvenirs.[9] These help CETs tell their story in a very concrete way, and are also very useful cues for starting conversations with people back home. Like the grain of sand around which a pearl forms, visuals give people a specific place to begin asking questions.

Many churches and individual Christians support CETs by helping them reproduce and distribute circular letters (prayer letters) through which they can share with family, friends, and other interested people about life in the host country. One of the greatest benefits of these letters is that they encourage CETs to begin thinking about and engaging in the task of interpreting long before they reach home. It is a shame only to use such letters as a convenient way to pass on personal news to a large audience because when writing such letters CETs have an excellent opportunity to begin reflecting on what they are learning in the host culture and how to explain these things to a home audience. Such letters are a vital part of the interpretation process. The personal connection between the CET and readers means that readers are likely to grant these letters a high level of attention and credibility. For CETs who are inclined toward writing articles for church magazines and the like, there is also much to be said for gathering information and beginning the writing process while still in the host country. Often during the process of writing, a CET will become aware of the need for additional information which is more easily accessible in the host country than it would be later at home.

Choosing and focusing messages: As with any other kind

of communication, CETs will generally have more success reaching and holding an audience if they focus the messages that they want to convey, and if they address questions that their audience can relate to.

One of the best ways for CETs to identify issues that would interest and edify home audiences is by maintaining a record of their own experience with the church in the host country, perhaps by keeping some kind of journal, and making note of those things that were interesting, exciting, challenging, or troubling. The disadvantage of CETs' starting with themselves is that if they are not careful they will present a view of the host church from their own perspective rather than presenting the host culture from its own perspective. However, CETs' own experience is likely to be a good guide as to what would be interesting and new to home audiences, and is thus often a good starting place as CETs ask themselves how to arouse the interest of home audiences and gain their attention. CETs also need to look inside themselves and ask the question: What have I learned? It is often the insights which CETs have gained through their personal transformation and spiritual growth in the host country that can be shared with conviction and passion.

Establishing credibility: As noted above, CETs cannot assume that people at home will automatically accept all that they have to say, especially if their message challenges popular opinion or belief. It is therefore necessary for CETs to be as credible as possible. The most basic way for CETs to establish credibility is to do their homework well, learning as much as possible about the church in the host country. Here it helps if CETs not only learn, but also gather information and organize it so that they can refer to it later. Memory fades quickly, and CETs will be much less effective as interpreters if their only data consists of vaguely remembered generalizations. The ability to present specific facts gives CETs much more credibility with audiences.

CETs also need to try to be as objective and fair in their portrayal of church life in the host culture as possible. Usually CETs have become personally involved in whatever

Christian work and churches they participated in, and want to support them in any way possible. With audiences at home CETs may be tempted to paint the host church in the most glowing terms possible. However, an overly rosy picture may seem too good to be true, and if it is obvious to listeners that CETs have no critical distance on what they describe, credibility may suffer. A frank but generally upbeat appraisal is often more effective in winning over an audience. (If CETs have had a very bad experience in the host country, there is also the possibility that they will err in the other direction, painting the work or the church in unfairly bleak terms, so if a CET's experience has not been good she or he needs to be especially cautious about reporting fairly.)

Finally, as CETs write and talk, they also need to stay within the limits of their own knowledge and experience—in other words, to make liberal use of "I don't know" when necessary. Many people at home will view CETs as experts in the host culture and its church, and it is very easy for CETs to be drawn into a greater expert role than they are prepared for. (There is a special temptation in addressing relatively uninformed audiences because it is easy for CETs to get away with making questionable assertions even when they really don't know what they are talking about.) Willingness to admit one's ignorance requires a degree of self-discipline, but it is very important for CETs to do this if they are to avoid having their credibility destroyed by being lured into some false statement—and then caught out publicly by an audience member who *is* informed.

Continued interpretation: After returning home, CETs will no doubt have opportunities through talks at church groups and other gatherings to share what they have learned about the church in their host country, although, CETs may need to be active in seeking such opportunities rather than waiting for them to present themselves. However, what CETs have learned in Christian churches abroad should ideally have an impact going beyond talks and presentations about the host country and its church. Such talks and presentations are good for encouraging home churches and highlighting a few carefully chosen points from the CET's experience. But it is rare for such opportunities to allow CETs to share in depth either their understanding of the host culture or new understandings they have of their own faith as a result of experience in the host culture. It is only as CETs integrate back into their home church community over time, participating in worship, prayer, Bible study, service, and the administrative life of the church, that they can gradually apply what they have learned to the life of their home churches.

During the months or years that CETs spend participating in the life of a Christian church in another country and culture, it is almost inevitable that CETs' own faith will be enriched and broadened. There is a great need in the church worldwide for more Christians who are able to see God from a perspective that is not confined by the narrow bounds of a single culture. Through experience in churches of other cultures CETs are in a position to make an important contribution toward meeting this need. CETs should see this learning and sharing as one of the most important aspects of their role. By helping Western churches better understand the situation of the Christian church in other countries, CETs can keep Western churches well informed as to how they might assist churches in other countries and support them in prayer, and can also help Western churches avoid some of the mistakes of past mission efforts. An enhanced understanding of the life of the church in other countries and cultures is also vitally important to the spiritual health of Western churches because churches which are cut off from the Christian experience of churches in other places all too easily become narrow and inbred. One of the best ways to find revitalization and broader perspective is by experiencing how God is working in different countries and cultures. This interpreter role is often not an easy one for CETs to play, but the contribution CETs make to Western churches by interpreting the experience of churches in other countries is vitally important if Christians worldwide are to work toward turning the idea of the church universal into a reality.

Conclusion

Throughout this book, the idea of reconciliation as a theme around which to discuss the Christian calling of CETs may have seemed somewhat peculiar to many readers as this is not the way in which the mission calling of CETs is normally discussed. However, I hope I have convinced readers that CETs do indeed have a special role to play in Christian mission, a role in reconciliation between churches of different cultures and traditions, between peoples of different nations and cultures, and between God and humankind, and that there are good reasons for Western churches to support mission efforts of this type.

Underlying this mission role is the paradox that in order to be effective in this mission of reconciliation, Christian English teachers must be learners as well as teachers. If CETs are to be effective mediators between their own culture and their host culture, they need to demonstrate their interest in and respect for the host culture through a sincere effort to learn about the host culture. Likewise, if CETs are to build better relations between churches of different cultures and traditions, churches which have often had weak or even adversarial relations in the past, it is necessary that they approach these churches with a learner posture which suggests not only a desire to learn but also genuine respect. Finally, if CETs' witness is to cause people to be more open to the kingdom of God, CETs must not only proclaim the gospel and live in such a way as to commend it, but also live in ways that convince people in the host culture that it is a good thing for people of different cultures to share with and learn from each other, even in matters as deeply rooted in identity and culture as faith. CETs will only be convincing in this latter message if they first open themselves up to the host culture as learners.

For Christians in mission, English teaching can and should be much more than an opportunity to gain access to closed nations for evangelistic purposes, or a form of social work only incidentally carried out by Christians. It can be an opportunity to bear witness, to minister, to serve the disadvantaged, to contribute toward peace between people of different cultures, and even to build better relations between different branches of the church universal. Looked at in these ways, English teaching can be more than a secular job that serves as a means to other ends—English teaching itself becomes a form of Christian mission.

Notes

CHAPTER 1: A CHRISTIAN VOCATION IN ITS OWN RIGHT

1. Seaman 2000.
2. Dickerson and Dow 1997:18-25, 29-39. As Dickerson and Dow note (28), the total number of organizations sending English teachers is no doubt even larger than their survey indicates ("EFL" stands for "English as a Foreign Language" and refers to the teaching of English in countries where English is not spoken as the native language.)
3. Seaman (2000) notes that even in 1910 the issue of English teaching and mission generated considerable controversy at the Edinburgh conference because of concern "that English language instruction would tend to associate Christianity with Anglo-Saxon culture, and that graduates of mission schools would become culturally separated from their own peoples."
4. A survey by Dickerson and Dow found that CETs were most likely to teach in Asia, especially China; many also work in recently ex-communist nations in Eastern Europe or countries that were until recently part of the Soviet Union. Most also teach adults at the college level. Dickerson and Dow 1997:40.
5. Noll 1994; Marsden 1997.

CHAPTER TWO: A SPECIAL ROLE FOR CHRISTIAN ENGLISH TEACHERS

1. Purgason 1998:33.
2. Shenk 1993:18.
3. See Bosch 1991:389-393 for discussion.
4. Hiebert 1985:263.
5. For more on the rise of English see Crystal 1997; also Phillips 1999, chapter 14.
6. I borrow the term "Anglo-America" from Phillips 1999. Phillips (604-607) argues that in a world of ethnocultural alignments, the United States and United Kingdom form one of the most important super-national groupings, with far closer ties to each other than to their other neighbors, and that this unity is symbolized in large part by their common language.
7. It was in schools within Britain's colonial empire, often mission schools, that the English language began to move beyond its base among the Anglo-

Saxon peoples toward becoming an international language. Seaman 2000.

8. Despite the fact that the Opium War took place over 150 years ago, memories of it are kept vigorously alive in Chinese school textbooks, television series, and films.

9. Hiebert 1994:57.

10. Seaman 2000.

11. Traditional Islamic thought does not recognize a distinction between faith and government—the ideal for Islamic polity was that the Islamic world would be under one leader combining religious and political functions.

12. See Bosch 1991:304-313 for discussion.

13. Fernando 1999:77.

14. Bosch 1991:290-294.

15. Horner 1993:168.

16. Kuzmic 1993:158

CHAPTER THREE: LEARNING AS WITNESS

1. Brewster and Brewster 1984:1.

2. Purgason 1998:34.

3. Grove and Torbiorn 1993:82; Barna 1994:343.

4. Furnham and Bochner 1986:124-125.

5. For further discussion of culture shock, see Kohls 1996:87-104. Hiebert 1985:64-89 provides a more detailed discussion directed specifically to Western missionaries, and Snow 1995:270-275 discusses the issue with regard to volunteer English teachers overseas.

6. I borrow this usage of the word "translating" from Sanneh 1989.

7. Newbigin 1986:4.

8. Sanneh 1989:51.

9. Sanneh contrasts Christianity with Islam, a religion which is tightly bound to a single (Arabic) culture. The contrast is perhaps most clearly evident in the sharply contrasting views the two religions hold toward translation of their scriptures. While Christians have actively promoted translation of the Bible into hundreds of languages, Muslims traditionally believe the Koran should not be translated from its native Arabic into any other language.

10. This long experience with the local culture can be a curse as well as a blessing—often the local culture comes to dominate the church. However, this is a problem which is by no means unique to non-Western churches.

11. Hiebert 1985:141.

12. Another reason CETs should learn about how the gospel has become incarnated in the local culture is that this may enhance their own spiritual growth. The issue of learning about the local church is addressed further in chapter 8.

13. As one conference participant pointed out to me, there is also often a special affinity between students and foreign teachers because both are relatively disempowered outsiders within the school community.

14. Payne 1995:33, citing Alvin Rubinstein and Donald Smith.

15. For more extended discussion of this point, see Brewster and Brewster 1984. Also, as Hiebert 1985:82 points out, when missionaries place themselves in a nonthreatening student role, this may increase the willingness of people to learn about them and hear what they have to say about their faith.

16. Marshall 1989 discusses language learning strategies working with tutors (mentors) in the host country. For further reading on language learning, see

Brown 1991 and Rubin and Thompson 1994; see also chapter 15 of Snow 1996. General resources for culture learning include Hess 1994 and 1997, and Darrow and Palmquist 1977

CHAPTER FOUR: ENGLISH TEACHING AS WITNESS

1. Scovel 1990:5.
2. For Christian ESL/EFL materials, see Eby 1990 and Dickerson and Dow 1997.
3. See Purgason 1998:33-34 for discussion of different models in which CETs work as parts of evangelistic teams. One example would be a model in which a camp is run by a team of local and Western Christians, with CETs serving as English teachers and evangelistic outreach carried out by either local Christians or foreign Christians who are more knowledgeable about the local language and culture. (Alan Seaman, personal communication.)
4. Good introductory books on language teaching include Brown 1994b; Cross 1991; and Hadley 1993. Snow 1996 is geared specifically to the needs of volunteer English teachers who have not undergone professional training. See Dickerson and Dow 1997:47-61 for a comprehensive list of books on language teaching.

For information about ESL programs in North America, see Garshick, Ellen, ed., 1998, *Directory of Professional Preparation Programs in TESOL in the United States and Canada, 1999-2001* (TESOL); for ESL programs in the United Kingdom see Griffith, Susan, 1999, *Teaching English Abroad*, 4th edition (Vacation Work). See Dickerson and Dow 1997:18-26 for a listing of ESL training programs offered by Christian institutions.
5. CETs who work in settings where public Christian witness is discouraged may take comfort from Paul's note in this passage that there is no law against a witness based on these traits.
6. For further discussion, see Wong 2000.
7. Purgason 1994:238.
8. See Newbigin 1986 for a book-length treatment of this issue. For critical examination of the theory that the origins of the United States are uniquely Christian, see Noll, Hatch, and Marsden 1983.
9. Purgason 1998:35.
10. Bosch 1991:138.
11. Newbigin 1991:2; 49.

CHAPTER FIVE: ENGLISH TEACHING AS MINISTRY

1. Bergen 1996.
2. For discussion of the relationship of language teaching practices to humanism, see Stevick 1990.
3. "EFL" stands for English as a foreign language, and refers to the teaching of English in countries where English is not the native language. This stands in contrast to "ESL"—English as a second language—which refers to teaching English in English-speaking countries (to immigrants, foreign students, and so forth).
4. Brown 1994b:27-28; 29.
5. One of the greatest advantages of team teaching arrangements in which a Western teacher and a local teacher work together is that (in theory at least) they present both teachers to students as equal partners.

6. Local teacher's memories of what it was like to learn English do not necessarily translate into compassionate approaches to teaching—in fact (like veterans the world over), local teachers may sometimes be subtly tempted to bolster their own position as successful learners by making the initiation process for newcomers rigorous, ensuring that the greenhorns pay their dues.

7. For CETs who have taught ESL in their home countries to immigrants, foreign students, and so forth, one of the main adjustments they may need to make when going abroad is to lower levels of student motivation. Students who are surrounded by an English-speaking environment—and who often have pressing need to learn English for work, study, or just daily survival—can more consistently be counted on for zeal in English study than can those who have relatively little immediate need for the language.

8. Actually, the first two kinds of rewards are given more attention in Western discussions of motivation than the third kind is, but I will argue below that this is because they fit better into Western cultural notions.

9. See Brown 1994a:155-157.

10. Brown 1994b:39.

11. For discussion of how to design courses so that students are more aware of progress, see Snow 1996:50-52, 54-58.

12. See Brown 1994b:42-44 for further discussion of ways to build students' intrinsic motivation.

13. Yang 1986:113-115.

14. Brown 1994b:39.

CHAPTER SIX: ENGLISH TEACHING AS CHRISTIAN SERVICE

1. Garrett 1994:615-616.

2. Covell 1995:275-276.

3. Stott 1975:26.

4. Stott 1975:23-24.

5. Of course, such exhortations are not only found in the ministry of Jesus. For example, James 2:14-17 mocks Christians who profess concern for the naked and hungry and pray for them, but never actually bestir themselves to provide clothing or food.

6. Matthew's version of the Beatitudes (5:3-10) uses the phrase "poor in spirit," but even in Matthew those characterized as blessed—the poor in spirit, the meek, and those who mourn—do not appear to be the wealthy and powerful.

7. Parry 1994:82.

8. McKay 1992:16-17; 36-38; Tollefson 1991:140.

9. Tollefson 1991:5.

10. McKay 1992:12-13.

11. McKay 1992:30.

12. This information is drawn from Crystal 1997, mainly chapter 4.

13. Phillipson 1992:5-6.

14. Tollefson 1991, Phillipson 1992, and Pennycook 1994 are all book-length presentations of this viewpoint.

15. Tollefson 1991:97.

16. Pennycook 1994:307-308.

17. The Amity Foundation is a Chinese nongovernment organization established by Chinese Protestant Church leaders in 1985 to carry out development projects in China with the assistance of church agencies around the world.

18. For a more general list of questions foreign English teachers should ask in a new country to ensure that their English teaching is relevant to a particular setting, see Snow 1996:54-58.

19. Hiebert 1994:251.

CHAPTER SEVEN: ENGLISH TEACHING TOWARD PEACEMAKING AND INTERCULTURAL UNDERSTANDING

1. See also Isaiah 53:4-5 and Colossians 1:19-23.

2. Volf 1996:126.

3. See also James 3:17-18.

4. Huntington 1996.

5. Bennett 1993:31.

6. For example, I am painfully aware of the overgeneralization I engage in by lumping great variety of cultures under the label "Western," but for the sake of efficiency I beg the reader's indulgence.

7. Gundykunst and Kim 1997:177.

8. For discussion of the importance of differentiated categories in intercultural sensitivity, see Bennett 1993.

9. Fantini 1997 and Tomalin and Stempelski 1993 are resources for teachers which contain many different activities for dealing with culture topics in EFL classes: Fantini also has a good bibliography of other resources. Levin and Adelman 1993 is a student textbook which contains lessons both about United States culture and intercultural interaction.

10. Samovar and Porter 1995:274.

11. Gundykunst and Kim 1997:177.

12. Gundykunst and Kim (1997:14) note that when talking about the behavior of others, people often make little distinction between their description of a situation (the visible facts) and their interpretation of it.

13. Samovar, Porter, and Jain 1981:62; Bennett 1993:60.

14. Bennett 1993:53.

15. Samovar and Porter 1995:274; Hiebert 1985:97.

16. For more information on critical incident exercises, see Wight 1995, Dant 1995, and Bennett 1995. Storti 1994 is a collection of critical incident dialogues in which Americans interact with people of other cultures. While not designed for English classes, these might be a helpful model for teachers writing critical incident exercises for English classes.

17. The provision of answers requires that teachers constructing ICS exercises do a fair amount of research to ensure that the "right" answer in fact represents the way most foreigners would view the encounter, thus making ICS exercises relatively time-consuming to construct. For a general introduction to ICS, see Albert 1995, Brislin 1995, Cushner and Brislin 1996, and Triandis 1995. Cushner and Brislin 1996 also provides a comprehensive set of exercises designed to prepare Westerners for interaction with people of other cultures, and these exercises could serve as useful models for CETs who wish to construct ICS exercises for students of English. Murphey 1994 contains ICS exercises designed specifically for students of English who are learning about American culture.

18. Brislin 1993:180; Gundykunst and Kim 1987:87.

19. This phenomenon is seen most clearly in the worldwide acceptance of patriotism as a virtue, despite the fact that it is essentially a grand form of the self-interest principle—when there is a conflict of interest between nations, a

patriotic standard almost inevitably means placing the interests of "our" nation above those of "others."
20. Sanneh 1989:202-203. See also Hiebert 1994, chapter 3.
21. Volf 1996:40.
22. Purgason (1998:37) emphasizes that evenhandedness is especially important when dealing with cultural issues that are related to faith.
23. Often questions to students about their culture can be turned into activities which give more students more language practice than simply asking the question would. For example, rather than just asking one or two students who the host country's greatest authors are, the teacher can put students in groups, have each group discuss and decide who the five most important writers in their country's history are, and then have each group report

CHAPTER EIGHT: ENGLISH TEACHERS AS BRIDGES BETWEEN CHURCHES
1. By way of example, one legacy of Western missions in China is that Protestant and Catholic Christianity are generally seen as two distinct and different religions, and in the Chinese language there is no widely used word for the concept of "Christian." The closest equivalent, *jidutu*, generally refers to Protestant Christians, *tianzhujiaotu* being the term for Catholic Christians. Hence Westerners in China sometimes hear the surprising question (in English): "Are you Christian or Catholic?"
2. Bosch 1991:456.
3. Bosch 1991:456.
4. Hiebert 1985:55.
5. Newbigin 1986:9.
6. In countries where the position of the Christian community is tenuous, and where a Westerner's presence in church would draw unwanted attention, local Christians may still feel obligated to welcome CETs, or at least not directly ask them to leave. It is therefore important in such countries that CETs listen carefully for indirect and hinted messages, and be gracious and understanding if it seems that a church would prefer that they not regularly attend.
7. My thanks to Kitty Purgason for pointing this out.
8. I remember one evangelistic service, consisting mainly of a sermon and altar call, that was conducted by a visiting United States group at a Chinese church I attended in Taiwan. The congregation was polite and friendly both during and after the service, and based on conversations after the service I am quite sure that, despite the fact nobody came forward for the altar call, the Americans felt the service went well.
What the Americans didn't realize was that the Chinese congregation that day consisted entirely of Christians, virtually all of whom had been Christians for many years. (In contrast, most of the American group—including the main speaker—were relatively recent converts.) The Americans left the church under the happy assumption that they had introduced the gospel to a group of Chinese to whom the gospel was relatively new. The Chinese were also pleased with the service—because the young American speaker had finally given up his sinful life and turned to Christ.
9. Slides and videotapes make for better group viewing, but also require equipment and setup time. Pictures can be pulled out and shown with less fuss during smaller informal gatherings. There is wisdom in having some of each.

Bibliography

Albert, Rosita
  1995   The intercultural sensitizer/cultural assimilator as a cross-cultural training method. In Fowler and Mumford 1995, pp. 157-167.

Athyal, Saphir
  1993   Southern Asia. In Phillips and Coote 1993, pp. 57-68.

Barna, Laray
  1994   Stumbling Blocks in Intercultural Communication. In Samovar and Porter 1994, pp. 337-346.

Barnlund, Dean
  1994   Communication in a global village. In Samovar and Porter 1994, pp. 26-35.

Bennett, Milton
  1993   Towards ethnorelativism: A developmental model of intercultural sensitivity. In Paige 1993, pp. 21-72.

Bennett, Milton
  1995   Critical incidents in an intercultural conflict-resolution exercise. In Fowler and Mumford 1995, pp. 147-156.

Bergen, Henry
  1996   Liberation through phonetics. In Cole 1996, pp. 57-60.

Bond, Michael, ed.
  1988   *The Psychology of the Chinese People*. Oxford University Press.

Bosch, David
  1991   *Transforming Mission*. Orbis.

Brewster, Thomas and Elizabeth
    1984   *Language Learning IS Communication—IS Ministry.*
            Lingua House.

Brislin, Richard
    1993   *Understanding Culture's Influence on Behavior.* Harcourt
            Brace.

Brislin, Richard
    1995   The culture-general assimilator. In Fowler and Mumford
            1995, pp. 169-178.

Brown, Douglas
    1991   *Breaking the Language Barrier.* Intercultural Press.

Brown, Douglas
    1994a   *Principles of Language Learning and Teaching,* 3rd ed.
            Prentice Hall Regents.

Brown, Douglas
    1994b   *Teaching by Principles: An Interactive Approach to
            Language Pedagogy.* Prentice Hall Regents.

Chrystal, David
    1997   *English as a Global Language.* Cambridge University Press.

Cole, Lois, ed.
    1996   *China Passages: An Amity Teachers Anthology.* The Amity
            Foundation.

Covell, Ralph
    1995   *The Liberating Gospel in China: The Christian Faith
            Among China's Minority Peoples.* Baker.

Cross, David
    1991   *A Practical Handbook of Language Teaching.* Cassell.

Cushner, Kenneth, and Richard Brislin
    1996   *Intercultural Interaction: A Practical Guide,* 2nd ed. Sage
            Publications.

Dant, William
    1995   Using critical incidents as a tool for reflection. In Fowler
            and Mumford 1995, pp. 141-146.

Darrow, Ken, and Brad Palmquist
    1977   *Trans-Cultural Study Guide,* 2nd ed. Volunteers in Asia.

Dickerson, Lonna, and Dianne Dow
    1997   *Handbook for Christian EFL Teachers.* Billy Graham
            Center, Wheaton College.

Eby, Wesley
    1990   *Handbook for Teaching Bible-Based ESL.* Publications
            International.

Fantini, Alvino, ed.
    1997   *New Ways in Teaching Culture.* TESOL.

Fernando, Ajith
    1999   Bombs away: How Western military actions affect the work of the church. In *Christianity Today*, June 14, 1999, pp. 76-77.

Fowler, Sandra, and Monica Mumford, eds.
    Intercultural Sourcebook: Cross-Cultural Training Methods, Vol. 1. Intercultural Press.

Furnham, Adrian, and Stephen Bochner
    1986   *Culture Shock: Psychological Reactions to Unfamiliar Environments.* Routledge.

Garrett, Laurie
    1994   *The Coming Plague: Newly Emerging Diseases in a World Out of Balance.* Penguin Books.

Gittins, Anthony
    1989   *Gifts and Strangers: Meeting the Challenge of Inculturation.* Paulist Press.

Grove, Cornelius, and Ingemar Torbiorn
    1993   A new conceptualization of intercultural adjustment and the goals of training. In Paige 1993, pp. 73-108.

Gundykunst, William, and Young Yun Kim
    1984   *Communicating with Strangers: An Approach to Intercultural Communication.* Random House.

Gundykunst, William, and Young Yun Kim
    1997   *Communicating with Strangers: An Approach to Intercultural Communication*, 3rd edition. McGraw Hill.

Hadley, Alice Omaggio
    1993   *Teaching Language in Context: Proficiency Oriented Instruction*, 2nd ed. Heinle and Heinle.

Hess, J. Daniel
    1994   *The Whole World Guide to Culture Learning.* Intercultural Press.

Hess, J. Daniel
    1997   *Studying Abroad/Learning Abroad.* Intercultural Press (Abridgement of Hess 1994.)

Hiebert, Paul
    1985   *Anthropological Insights for Missionaries.* Baker.

Hiebert, Paul
    1994   *Anthropological Reflections on Missiological Issues.* Baker.

Hill, Clifford, and Kate Parry, eds.
1994   *From Testing to Assessment: English as an International Language.* Longman.

Huntington, Samuel
1996   *The Clash of Civilizations and the Remaking of World Order.* Simon and Schuster.

Kohls, Robert
1996   *Survival Kit for Overseas Living*, 3rd ed. Intercultural Press.

Kuzmic, Peter
1993   Europe. In Phillips and Coote 1993, pp. 148-163.

Levine, Deena, and Mara Adelman
1993   *Beyond Language: Cross-Cultural Communication*, 2nd ed. Prentice Hall Regents.

McKay, Sandra
1992   *Teaching English Overseas: An Introduction.* Oxford University Press.

Marsden, George
1997   *The Outrageous Idea of Christian Scholarship.* Oxford University Press.

Marshall, Terry
1989   *The Whole World Guide to Language Learning.* Intercultural Press.

Moreau, Scott, ed.
2000   *Evangelical Dictionary of World Missions.* Baker Books.

Murphey, Andrew
1994   *Cultural Encounters in the USA: Cross-Cultural Dialogues and Mini-Dramas.* National Textbook Company.

Newbigin, Lesslie
1986   *Foolishness to the Greeks: The Gospel and Western Culture.* Eerdmans.

Newbigin, Lesslie
1991   *Truth to Tell: The Gospel as Public Truth.* Eerdmans.

Noll, Mark
1994   *The Scandal of the Evangelical Mind.* Eerdmans.

Noll, Mark, Nathan Hatch, and George Marsden
1983   *The Search for Christian America*, expanded ed. Helmers and Howard.

Paige, Michael, ed.
1993   *Education for the Intercultural Experience*, 2nd ed. Intercultural Press.

Parry, Kate
    1994   The test and the text: Readers in a Nigerian secondary
            school. In Hill and Parry 1994, pp. 82-113.

Payne, Richard
    1995   The Clash with Distant Cultures: Values, Interests, and
            Force in American Foreign Policy. State University of New
            York Press.

Pennycook, Alastair
    1994   The Cultural Politics of English as an International
            Language. Longman.

Phillips, James, and Robert Coote, eds.
    1993   Toward the 21st Century in Christian Mission. Eerdmans.

Phillips, Kevin
    1999   The Cousin's Wars: Religion, Politics, and the Triumph of
            Anglo-America. Basic Books.

Phillipson, Robert
    1992   Linguistic Imperialism. Oxford University Press.

Purgason, Kitty
    1994   In the workshop: How to communicate values and truth in
            the context of teaching English as a second or foreign lan-
            guage. Evangelical Missions Quarterly. July, pp. 238-243.
    1998   Teaching English to the world: Options and opportunities.
            International Journal of Frontier Missions. Vol. 15:1,
            pp. 33-39.

Rubin, Joan, and Irene Thompson
    1994   How to Be a More Successful Language Learner, 2nd ed.
            Heinle and Heinle.

Samovar, Larry, Richard Porter, and Nemi Jain
    1981   Understanding Intercultural Communication. Wadsworth.

Samovar, Larry, and Richard Porter, eds.
    1994.   Intercultural Communication: A Reader, 7th ed. Wads-
            worth.

Samovar, Larry, and Richard Porter.
    1995   Communication Between Cultures, 2nd ed. Wadsworth.

Sanneh, Lamin
    1989   Translating the Message: The Missionary Impact on
            Culture. Orbis.

Scovel, Thomas
    1990   Some theological reflections on English teaching in Japan.
            Unpublished text of address at YMCA in Gotemba, Japan.

Seaman, Alan
2000   Teaching English to speakers of other languages (TESOL). In Moreau 2000.

Snow, Don
1996   *More Than a Native Speaker: An Introduction for Volunteers Teaching Abroad.* TESOL.

Stevick, Earl
1990   *Humanism in Language Teaching.* Oxford University Press.

Storti, Craig
1994   *Cross-Cultural Dialogues: 74 Brief Encounters with Cultural Difference.* Intercultural Press.

Tollefson, James
1991   *Planning Language Inequality.* Longman.

Tomalin, Barry, and Susan Stempleski
1993   *Cultural Awareness.* Oxford University Press.

Triandis, Harry
1995   Culture-specific assimilators. In Fowler and Mumford 1995, pp. 179-186.

Volf, Miroslav
1996   *Exclusion and Embrace: A Theological Exploration of Identity, Otherness, and Reconciliation.* Abingdon.

Weaver, Gary
1993   Understanding and coping with cross-cultural adjustment stress. In Paige 1993, pp. 137-168.

Wight, Albert
1995   The critical incident as a training tool. In Fowler and Mumford 1995, pp. 127-140.

Wong, Mary Shepard
2000   *The Influence of Gender and Culture on the Pedagogy of Five Western ESL Teachers in China.* Unpublished doctoral dissertation.

Yang Kuo-shu
1986   Chinese personality and its change. In Bond 1986, pp. 106-160.

The Author

Don Snow has degrees from the College of Wooster (B.A., history), Michigan State University (M.A., Teaching English as a second language), and Indiana University (Ph.D., East Asian Languages and Cultures). He has taught English at a number of institutions in Taiwan, Hong Kong, the Chinese mainland, and U.S., and has served with a number of organizations that send English teachers abroad, including the YMCA, Educational Services International (formerly Educational Services Exchange with China), and the United Board for Christian Higher Education in Asia.

Don is currently a mission co-worker of the Presbyterian Church (USA), and seconded by them to the Overseas Coordination office of the Amity Foundation, a Chinese nongovernmental development organization established by Chinese Christians. At Amity, Don works with the Teachers Project, a program through which teachers from more than a dozen nations in Europe, North America, and Asia are invited to serve as foreign language teachers in China. Don and his wife, Wei Hong Snow, live in Hong Kong.

CPSIA information can be obtained at www.ICGtesting.com
Printed in the USA
LVOW10s0256220116

471801LV00028B/363/P